A Year of Children's Sermons

A Year of Children's Sermons

Leon W. Castle

BROADMAN PRESS
Nashville, Tennessee

© Copyright 1976 • Broadman Press
All rights reserved

ISBN: 0-8054-4918-3
4249-18

Dewey Decimal Classification: 252
Subject heading: CHILDREN'S SERMONS

Library of Congress Catalog Card Number: 76-6717
Printed in the United States of America

to my family
Nancy, Lonnie, Karen, Kristie

Preface

In recent months much attention has been focused on the child and his worship experience within a church. At long last, children are being recognized as important participants in the corporate worship experience. This has not always been true. Too many times in the past, the entire worship experience was directed totally to the adults in the congregation. Children became detached and merely tolerated the hour. As a result many children have learned at an early age to "tune out" during the period that has excluded them in content and approach. The thoughtful worship planner is asking, "When will the child, as he grows and develops, tune back into a vital worship experience planned for the entire family?"

The "children's sermon" is a viable means of involving boys and girls in the corporate worship experience. Children's sermons based on favorite Bible stories will uniquely involve boys and girls in the worship service of the church.

No one is better equipped to write such a book on this subject than the author, Leon Castle. A recognized religious educator and leader in the field of childhood education, Mr. Castle blends basic Christian doctrine with sound educational principles. He draws from a rich background which includes experience as minister of education and minister of childhood education in various churches. This experience has equipped him with a very practical and workable approach. He has also written curriculum materials for children for a number of years and now serves as consultant in Children's work in the Sunday School Department of the Baptist Sunday School Board.

Mr. Castle has effectively involved hundreds of boys and girls in children's sermons during worship services at Glorieta and Ridgecrest Baptist Conference Centers. Through these experiences literally hundreds of pastors have asked for a book to aid them in planning children's sermons. From these requests have come this book.

Robert G. Fulbright

Introduction

Materials in this book may be used in a variety of ways. The primary intent of the book, however, is to provide materials for worship leaders to use in "children's worship features" during the regular worship services of the church.

A children's worship feature is the time during the worship service when the worship leader focuses his complete attention upon the children in the congregation. The feature should be a regular part of the order of service.

Various approaches may be used effectively.

- Many worship leaders call the children to the front of the meeting place. The children may sit around the one leading the feature. The leader should sit so all the children can see him. The children may stand around the leader rather than sit. In this case, the leader should stand so all the children can see him.

- Some worship leaders reserve the front rows of the meeting place for children to sit. The worship leader stands in front of but close to the children during the feature.

- Worship leaders often prefer that the children remain seated with their parents. The leader in this case conducts the worship feature from the pulpit.

The feature may be scheduled at any time during the service. Each leader will need to determine the best time for the feature. Many leaders find that toward the beginning of the service is the most ideal time.

Whenever, wherever, and however the feature is conducted,

remember that it is for children. Therefore remarks should be addressed to them. Speak to needs and interests that children have. It is not the time to say something to the adults through the disguise of speaking to children.

Speak the language of children. They are literalists. They will interpret what you say concretely and literally. Therefore, say what you mean and mean what you say. The "language of Zion" does not say to children what it says to adults. Children best understand short, one- and two-syllable words. Their vocabulary is primarily composed of such words. Remember this when you speak to them.

Look at the children as you talk to them. If possible, sit or stand so you can see the eyes of every child. Eye contact is necessary for the most effective communication.

Make the feature a two-way street. Do not do all the talking. Allow the children to respond. Get them involved.

The adult who desires to help meet spiritual needs of children will find many uses for this book. Consider using the contents for children's worship programs, devotionals for children, bedtime stories for children, or family worship times.

Acknowledgments

Scripture quotations marked TLB are from *The Living Bible, Paraphrased* (Wheaton: Tyndale House Publishers, 1971) and are used by permission.

The Bible stories in the following sermons are adapted as indicated and are used by permission.

2—adapted from *Bible Discoverers,* April, May, June, 1973. © Copyright 1973, The Sunday School Board of the Southern Baptist Convention. All rights reserved.

3—adapted from *13 Worship Programs for Grades 1 Through 3,* Broadman Supplies.

7, 9, 16, 21, 27, 46—adapted from *Children's Leadership,* January, February, March, 1976. © Copyright 1975, The Sunday School Board of the Southern Baptist Convention. All rights reserved.

8, 13, 14, 15, 20—adapted from *Exploring the Bible,* teacher's edition (Convention Press, 1972), pp. 55, 61, 62, 78-79, 86.

12—adapted from *Exploring the Bible,* pupil's edition (Convention Press, 1972), pp. 9-11.

40—adapted from *Bible Discoverers: Teacher,* January, February, March, 1976. © Copyright 1975, The Sunday School Board of the Southern Baptist Convention. All rights reserved.

Contents

God

1. God Gives 15
2. God Cares 17
3. God Creates 19
4. God Loves 20
5. God Forgives 22

Jesus

6. Jesus Was Loving 25
7. Jesus Was Helpful 27
8. Who Is Jesus? 29
9. Jesus Was Kind 31
10. Jesus Was Friendly 33
11. Jesus Was Forgiving 35

Bible

12. The Bible Is About God 37
13. What Is the Bible? 39
14. God's Word Is a Guidebook 42
15. God's Word Is Eternal 43
16. God's Word Is Powerful 46

Church

17. The Church Tells About Jesus 48
18. The Church Prays Together 50
19. The Church Has Leaders 52
20. What Is the Church? 53
21. The Church Helps People 56

Self

22. I Can Become 58
23. I Am Special 60
24. I Have Abilities 62
25. I Can Improve 64

Friends

26. Friends Depend on Each Other 66
27. Friends Help Each Other 68
28. Friends Rejoice Together 70
29. Friends Love at All Times 72
30. Friends Are Loyal and True 74
31. Friends Are Friendly 76

Home and Family

32. Forgiving My Family 78
33. Living Peaceably with My Family 80
34. Being Obedient to My Parents 82
35. Being Helpful to My Family 84

Relationships

36. Learning About Sharing 87
37. Learning About Kindness 89
38. Learning About Honesty 91
39. Learning About Caring for the Body 93
40. Learning to Accept Authority 95
41. Thou Shalt Not Covet 97
42. Learning About Doing One's Best 99
43. Learning About Heroes 102
44. Learning About Fears 104
45. Learning About Jealousy 106
46. Learning About Mercy 108

Special Days

47. Thanking God for Mothers 110
48. O Give Thanks 112
49. He Is Alive 114
50. Learning the Meaning of Christmas 116
51. The Beginning of a Nation 118
52. Thanking God for Fathers 120

A Year of Children's Sermons

God

1
God Gives

Preparation: Study the Sermon on the Mount, Matthew 5—7. Find a large red apple. Polish it.

Sermon: Show the apple to the children. Ask: "What do I hold in my hand? How are apples used?"

Listen for the word *eat*. Talk about the various ways apples can be used as food.

Ask: "Do you ever worry about what you will eat? Do you ever worry about what you will drink and what clothes you will wear? Do you ever worry about anything?

"Friends of Jesus worried. Listen to hear what Jesus told them."

Jesus was talking with a large group of his friends. He knew they worried about many things. They worried about having clothes to wear, food to eat, and clean water to drink.

These friends have no cause for worry, Jesus could have thought. How can I help them believe that God, my father, will care for them?

Jesus looked around. Beautiful red lilies grew wild on the hillside where they sat. Little birds flew through the air and rested in the trees.

He called the attention of the group to those objects of nature.

"Do not worry about things—what to eat, what to drink, and what to wear," he said. "Look at the birds. They do not sow seeds, harvest a crop, or store that harvest in a barn. They do not do those things because God, your heavenly Father, takes care of them.

"Listen! You are much more valuable to God than are the birds. Therefore, if God cares for them, will he not also take care of you?

"Worry all you wish, but worry will not add one single minute to your life.

"Why do you worry about your clothes? Look at all of these beautiful field lilies. They do not work weaving cloth and making clothes. Yet King Solomon, who was extremely wealthy and well dressed, did not wear clothes as beautiful as they.

"If God so cares for the flowers that live for such a very short while, will he not also take care of you?

"So, do not worry. Do not say, 'What are we going to have to eat? What are we going to have to drink? Or, what are we going to have to wear?' Those who do not believe in God talk like that.

"God, your heavenly Father, knows that you need food to eat. He knows that you must have water to drink and clothes to wear. He will gladly give them to you if you will try hard to do the things that are right.

"So do not worry about tomorrow. God will take care of you tomorrow just as he has cared for you today. Live one day at a time."

Response: Did Jesus think that a person should worry? Why not?

Remember this Bible verse, "God shall supply all your need" (Phil. 4:19).

Prayer: Thank you, God, for promising to take care of all our needs. Amen.

2
God Cares

Preparation: Study Psalm 23.

Meditate on God's care for you.

Find a live pet, caged or otherwise, that you can show the children. If that is impossible find a large picture of one.

Sermon: Show the pet to the children. Talk about what it is and things that have to be done to care for it. Ask: "Do you have a pet? Do you take care of it?"

Say, "I will tell you a story about a sheep. I will pretend to be the sheep. Listen for all the things the good shepherd does for his flock."

I am a sheep. I belong to my good shepherd, David.

I never worry about something to eat. My shepherd David always finds nice, big fields of green, juicy grass for me.

David always knows what is best for me. He knows that the day begins to get very hot by about 10:00 in the morning. I get thirsty and tired. But David knows that if I get hot and drink water with my stomach full, I will get sick. He makes me lie down and rest. Since I cannot eat lying down I will not overeat and become ill.

Poison plants and plants with sharp points that can stick into my nose grow in the grass. However, I never fear because David goes before me, digs those plants out of the ground, and burns them.

I am very much afraid of swift, running water. If I were to fall into the stream, my thick coat of wool would become so heavy that I would sink. Besides, I am not a good swimmer.

David always takes me to ponds and pools of still water. He may even use rocks to dam up a mountain stream in order to make a pool from which I will not be afraid to drink.

I do not see very well and I get lost easily. But I am never afraid to go out, for my shepherd always leads me to the places he wants me to go. He knows all the good paths.

I am very helpless and cannot protect myself. Sometimes danger threatens our flock but we are never afraid of it. David is with us. I remember times when lions and bears tried to catch us sheep. David used his heavy rod to kill them. If I were to fall over the edge of a mountain trail, David could catch me with the end of his shepherd crook and pull me back to safety. I feel safe with him to protect me.

I enjoy being near David. I like to rub against his robe. He pats my head and rubs my ears. I know his voice and when he speaks even though I do not see him, I know he is there.

It is wonderful to have a shepherd like David.

Response: Ask: "Was David a good shepherd? How?

"Just like David cared for his sheep, so does God care for us. How does he care for you? What does he give you?"

Prayer: Thank you, God, for taking care of us. In Jesus' name, amen.

3
God Creates

Preparation: Saturate yourself with the creation story found in Genesis 1.

Sermon: Say: "Boys and girls, I want you to help me tell the story today. When I say, 'and God said,' I want you to respond by saying, 'that's good.' Let's practice."
Leader: "And God said."
Children: "That's good."

Once upon a time long ago, soft white clouds did not float through a beautiful blue sky. Birds did not fly in the air or make nests in the trees. There was neither sky, air, clouds nor trees.

Grass did not grow on hills or in valleys. In fact, there were no hills or valleys.

Beautiful flowers did not grow from tiny seeds and bloom into lovely blossoms because there were no seeds.

Fish did not swim in the creeks, streams, lakes, or seas because neither fish nor water existed.

Children did not play in water puddles; they did not enjoy feeling soft mud ooze between their bare toes. Boys and girls did not make mud pies and leave them in the sunshine to dry. At that time, there were no boys, no girls, no mud, no sunshine.

Before the beginning there was nothing but darkness and emptiness—and God. The Bible tells us, "In the beginning God." God has always existed.

The first verse in Genesis says, "In the beginning God created the heavens and the earth."

God made the light and called it day. The dark he called night, and God said . . .

CHILDREN: That's good.

LEADER: God made the sky, the dry land, the oceans, and the seas. He made the grass, the flowers, the herbs, and the fruit trees. And God said . . .

CHILDREN: That's good.

LEADER: God made the sun, the moon, and the stars. He made the birds, the great whales, the fishes both big and small. And God said . . .

CHILDREN: That's good.

LEADER: God made the cattle and all the animals that walk upon the earth. And God said . . .

CHILDREN: That's good.

LEADER: Finally everything was ready for a man to be made. "So God created man in his own image, in the image of God created he him; male and female created he them" (Gen. 1:27). And God said . . .

CHILDREN: That's good.

Response: Ask: "What did God think about the things he made? (*They are good.*)

"Boys and girls, everything that God makes is good. In fact, everything that God does is good. Let us thank God for being and doing good."

Prayer: Ask the children to sing with you, "God Is So Good."

4
God Loves

Preparation: Study Luke 19:1-10.
Think of God's great love for you and thank him for it.

God/21

Sermon: Ask, "Have you ever heard the statement, 'If you do that God will not love you.' Listen to this story and decide whether or not that statement is true."

My name is Zacchaeus. I am a tax collector. In fact I am the chief tax collector.

I am a very rich man. Let me tell you how I got my wealth.

We tax collectors have an agreement with the Roman government. All the money we can collect over and above the requirements of the government, we can keep.

You can understand why the Jewish people are not especially fond of us.

Jesus came through Jericho one day. Great crowds gathered everywhere Jesus went. Today was no exception.

I had heard about Jesus, and I wanted to see who he was. But people crowded in front of me and blocked my view which made it impossible for me to see Jesus. You see I am short.

What can I do to see Jesus? I thought.

Suddenly I remembered the big sycamore tree that shaded the road over which Jesus would walk. That is a good spot for me. No one can get in front of me if I am in the tree. I will be able to see Jesus.

I ran in front of the crowd, climbed the tree, sat down on a limb, and waited for Jesus.

Soon I saw the man I had wanted so much to see. Jesus came walking down the road. When he got to the tree, he stopped. He looked up at me and said, "Zacchaeus!" Now how did he know my name? "Zacchaeus," he said, "quick! Come down out of the tree. I am going home with you. I must be a guest in your home today."

I could hardly believe what I heard. Jesus going home with me—a despised, hated tax collector. Why would he choose me over the many Jewish priests who lived here in Jericho?

Hurriedly, I came down the tree. Oh, the thrill I felt as I took Jesus to my house.

However, not everyone shared my excitement and joy. The crowd grew angry. They grumbled and murmured. "Why has Jesus gone home with Zacchaeus? Zacchaeus is a sinner and a famous one at that," they complained.

Jesus' love for me made a difference in my life that day. I became ashamed of myself. I regretted having stolen from the people. I stood before Jesus and said: "Lord, I will take half of everything that I own and give it to the poor. And if I find I have charged anyone too much on his taxes, I will give him back four times as much as I overcharged." That pleased Jesus. He said, "Today salvation has come to your house."

Response: Ask, "Did Jesus love Zacchaeus even though Zacchaeus did things that he should not have done?

"Boys and girls, God does you the same way. God's loving you does not depend on your being good. God loves you the way you are because he is just that way."

Prayer: Thank you, God, for loving us just as we are. Amen.

5
God Forgives

Preparation: Study Luke 15:11-32.
Thank God for being a forgiving Father.

Sermon: Ask: "Have you ever disobeyed your parents? How did you feel? How did your parents feel?

God/23

"Our story is about a son who disobeyed. Listen to learn what the father did about it."

A man had two sons.

The younger son wanted to leave home. He went to his father and said, "Dad, give me the part of my inheritance that I will get at your death." The father agreed and divided his wealth between his two sons.

A few days later, the younger son prepared to leave home. He gathered all his belongings, packed them, and left. He traveled to a distant country.

There the young son very carelessly and unwisely spent his wealth. He wasted all he had.

Then a famine came. Food became scarce and expensive. What would the young son do? He had no money. He had no friends. Soon he began to suffer extreme hunger.

The once wealthy, free-spender sought a job. He probably looked, asked, and begged for employment but could find none. Finally, he persuaded a local farmer to hire him as a farm helper.

The farmer gave the young son a very unpleasant job. The boy's responsibility was to feed pigs.

How terrible! Feeding pigs made the boy even more hungry. His hunger became so intense that he wanted to eat the pods he fed the pigs.

Hungry and alone he thought about his father, his brother, the home he left, and the servants that used to serve him.

"The servants back at home eat better than I do. Why should I stay here and suffer? I'll go back home. I'll ask my father to let me live like a servant not as a son."

Having made that decision, the young man started homeward.

I can suppose that his heart beat faster as he neared the home-place. His mind probably filled with questions. Wonder what Dad will say? What will he do? Will he let me come home or will he send me away? I wonder . . ."

Far down the road, a man came running toward the young son. Carefully the son looked. Suddenly, it dawned upon him that the man was his father.

What shall I do? he must have reasoned. Shall I run away? Shall I run toward him?

"My son! my son!" the father shouted. With arms extended the father joyfully met his wayward son, threw his arms around him, hugged and kissed him, and cried tears of great joy. What happiness the father experienced to once again see a son he thought he might never see again.

"Father, I have done you wrong. I have sinned against God. Please do not call me a son," the boy began.

"Hush! hush! my son," the father commanded. Turning to a servant, he said, "Bring a robe and put it upon my son. Put shoes on his feet and a ring on his finger. Kill the special calf and prepare it for a feast. For this my son who was lost is found. He who was dead is alive again."

Response: Ask, "How did the father feel toward the disobedient son? (*He loved him and forgave him.*)

"Boys and girls, God is like the father in the story. He is sad when we disobey him, but he is always willing to forgive when we say we are sorry. Isn't God good?"

Prayer: Sing, "God Is So Good."

Jesus

6
Jesus Was Loving

Preparation: Read Matthew 19:13-22. Think of ways children can express genuine love to others.

From red poster paper, cut a large heart.

Sermon: Show the large red heart. Ask, "What do you think of as you look at this heart?" Listen for the word *love*. Say: "I heard someone say *love*. Do any of you love someone? Does someone love you? Do people who love each other have ways of showing or expressing their love to each other?

"Listen to this story about Jesus. All of the details in the story are not told in the Bible. Some of them are what I think may have happened. When I finish tell me whether or not Jesus was a loving person."

All the ladies of the community gathered at the village well to draw water. They talked about Jesus and what they had heard about him.

"I want to take my baby to see Jesus. I want Jesus to touch him and bless him," one mother said.

Others wanted to do the same thing.

Many people surrounded Jesus the day the mothers took their children to see him. The mothers had to push their ways through the crowd.

Suddenly, they were stopped.

Jesus' disciples thought that Jesus was much too busy to be bothered with a group of little children.

"Stop," they said. "Do not come any closer. Do not bother Jesus. Can you not see that he is busy and has no time for you?" the disciples questioned.

Jesus saw what had happened. He became very provoked at the disciples. "Let the little children come to me, do not ever send them away," Jesus said.

One by one the mothers brought their little ones to Jesus. He took them up in his arms and loved them. He put his hands on them and gave them his blessing.

"Learn a lesson," he instructed the disciples. "The kingdom of God belongs to them. Whoever does not have their kind of faith will never enter the kingdom of God."

Shortly thereafter a young man hurried to Jesus.

"Good Master," he said as he knelt in the road before Jesus, "What must I do to get into the kingdom of heaven?"

"You know the commandments—live a pure life. Do not kill. Do not steal. Do not tell lies. Honor your father and mother," was Jesus' reply.

"Good teacher, all of those I have obeyed since I was a child."

Jesus watched the questioning young man. He loved him. "One more thing you need to do. Sell everything you have and give all your money to the poor," Jesus said lovingly.

Sadly the young man walked away for he was very rich.

Response: Ask: "Was Jesus loving? How?

"Think with me. Will you name three ways to show love to someone. (*Give adequate time for response.*)

"Sometimes saying I love you or showing love is very difficult to do. Let's ask God to help us."

Prayer: Dear God, help each of us to be able to say to someone this week, "I love you." Help us to say that to you. Thank you for sending Jesus who has showed us how to be loving. In his name we pray. Amen.

7
Jesus Was Helpful

Preparation: Study John 2:1-12.

Call one of the children in your congregation and ask to borrow a bride doll. Go by the home, visit with the child, and share your plans with the child.

Sermon: Ask: "Has your mother or father ever said, 'will you help me?' What about your schoolteacher? Has a friend ever asked you for help? Did you help? Have you ever helped someone without being asked?"

Show the bride doll. Say, "Look at this doll. Isn't she pretty? What kind of doll is she?

"Brides and weddings go together, do they not?

"I will tell you a story about a wedding when something went wrong. Someone needed help. Someone who attended a wedding proved to be very helpful. Listen to the story and discover what went wrong and who helped."

Jesus and his disciples attended a wedding in Cana in Galilee. Mary the mother of Jesus was also there.

During the wedding celebration the wine ran out. To run out of refreshments during such a joyous occasion was embarrassing. Mary became concerned and told Jesus what had happened.

Turning to the servants, Mary said, "Whatever he tells you to do, do it."

Six huge water jars that held about twenty gallons of water each sat nearby. The water from the pots was used to clean the feet of the guests before they went into the house and to wash their hands before and during meals.

Jesus said to the servants: "Fill the water pots with water. Fill them up to their tops."

The servants obeyed.

"Now dip out the drink and take it to the head waiter," Jesus said.

After tasting the drink, the head waiter sent for the bridegroom. The water had become wine. Not knowing the source of the wine, the head waiter said to the bridegroom, "Most men serve the best wine first, but you have kept the best until now."

Response: Ask: "What went wrong at the wedding? Who became the helper? How did he help?"

Ask the children to bow their heads and close their eyes. Say: "Think about your home. Can you be like Jesus and help your mother, father, brothers, and sisters? Think about school. Can you be like Jesus and in some way help your teacher, a classmate? Think about your friends. Can you be like Jesus and help them some way?"

Prayer: Dear God, thank you for sending Jesus to show us how to live. Help us to be helpful like he was helpful. In his name we pray. Amen.

8
Who Is Jesus?

Preparation: Read the Gospels. Reread John 1:1-18.
Clarify in your own mind your feelings and beliefs about Jesus.

Sermon: Lead the group to sing "Jesus Loves Me."

Ask the following questions. How old is Jesus? Where did Jesus come from? Did Jesus make anything? Was Jesus a man? How did people react to Jesus? What does Jesus tell us about God? Where is Jesus now?

Say, "The story I will now tell you about Jesus will answer those questions. Listen carefully."

If we could get into a space machine and travel back into time and go back as far as we could go—to the time when things were being created—guess who we would find? We would find Jesus. John said that in the beginning Jesus was there. Jesus has always been ever since before time began.

Since Jesus has always been nobody really knows where he came from.

Jesus' special friend, John, wrote in his Gospel that Jesus was the one who made everything.

He said that Jesus was God and was with God in the beginning. But Jesus was also a man. He came to earth as a human being. He was the promised Savior about whom the Old Testament spoke.

One day an angel visited a young woman in Nazareth whose name was Mary. The angel told Mary that she was going to have a special baby boy and that she was to name him Jesus. He was to be the Savior for that is what the name Jesus means.

As the angel had said, Mary had a baby boy and she called him Jesus.

Jesus was a real baby like babies today. Jesus was once a little boy just as real as you boys in this room today. Jesus became a teenager and was a real teenager just like real teenagers today. Jesus became a man and he was a man just as real as men are real today. Jesus ran and played, he laughed, he cried, he fell down and hurt himself. He loved his mother and Joseph just like you love your parents. He went to school, he learned. Jesus was really a human being. Jesus really did become a man.

For many, many years the Hebrews had been looking for Jesus, God's Son. But most of the Hebrews did not recognize Jesus as being God's Son. They thought that God's Son would be a king and have an army that would defeat all the nations of the world and make the Hebrews the world rulers.

But Jesus did not become an earthly king. Therefore, many people did not believe that he was God's Son.

When Jesus began to tell people that he was God's Son, it made some of them mad. When Jesus told some how God wanted them to live, it made them mad. Some became so mad at Jesus that they had him crucified or killed.

While Jesus lived on earth, he told people many things about God. Jesus said "I am God" and he was. He said, "If you want to know what God is like, look at me."

Jesus loved people. He was good and kind to them. He did good things for them and wanted the very best to happen to everybody. Jesus said that God is that way too.

Jesus said that he came to the world so that people might come to know God better. He came to the world so that people might love God better. He came to the world so that people would become sorry for doing things that God did not want them to do. He came to the world so that people would want to try their best to do what God wanted them to do.

After Jesus died on the cross, he was buried. But he did not stay dead. On the third day he rose from the dead. He stayed on earth for forty days and then went back to be with God. He is with God today, everywhere God is.

Response: Ask the children to bow their heads. Ask the pianist or organist to play something very softly. Lead the group in a prayer thanking God for sending Jesus.

9
Jesus Was Kind

Preparation: Read Luke 17:11-19.

Sermon: Say, "I am thinking about a Bible verse that says 'Be ye kind one to another.' Say that verse with me.

"Were any of you kind to someone last week? How were you kind? (Allow time for response.)

"Listen to the story that I will tell you about Jesus and decide whether or not Jesus was kind."

Leprosy was a dreaded skin disease. It meant almost certain death for the person who contacted the disease because there was no known cure for it. Death because of leprosy was slow and painful, many times taking twenty to thirty years to run its course.

Anyone who had the disease was called a leper.

He was required to tear his clothes and let his hair hang loose. A leper had to wear a mask-like covering over his mouth and upper lip. When anyone came near him he was to cry, "Unclean, unclean."

No one was supposed to come closer than eighteen inches to a leper. Furthermore, merely saying hello to a leper was against the law.

A leper was not allowed to approach another person. No leper was permitted to go into the city of Jerusalem or any other walled city.

If in the rare event, one was cured of his leprosy, he was required to report to a priest for an examination. If the priest confirmed the cure, an elaborate ceremony of sacrifice followed. The priest then issued a certificate stating that the leper was cleansed.

Jesus was on his way to Jerusalem. Outside a small village, he saw ten men grouped together. The men were lepers.

They were not permitted to go near anyone. However, these lepers broke the rules when they recognized Jesus.

Surely they must have heard about him. Do you suppose that they heard that Jesus did not like for people to be sick and that he had made many sick people well. Perhaps they had heard that Jesus had healed a leper.

Instead of crying, "Unclean, unclean," those lepers cried: "Jesus, master, have mercy on us. Jesus, master, have mercy on us."

Turning to the lepers Jesus said, "Go and show yourself to the priest."

Into the village they went. And while they were on their way to find a priest, a wonderful thing happened. The hurting, ugly sores began to disappear. Soon no sores remained and their skin was healthy and clean.

One of the men was overjoyed.

"Thank you, God. Thank you, oh thank you," he shouted.

I must thank Jesus, he thought.

Quickly he ran back to Jesus. Falling down on the ground in front of Jesus the leper said: "Thank you, thank you, Jesus, for making me well. Thank you for giving me clean, healthy skin again."

Jesus said to him, "Get up. You may go anywhere now. Your faith made you well."

Response: Ask: "Was Jesus kind? What did he do?

"Jesus wants us to be like him. To be like him, we must be kind.

"Do you find that it is always easy to be kind?

"Let's ask God to help us."

Prayer: Dear God, we want to be kind like Jesus was kind. But we find that being kind is sometimes hard to do. Help us to show kindness to someone this week. In Jesus' name, amen.

10
Jesus Was Friendly

Preparation: Read John 4 to review the story of Jesus and the Samaritan woman.

Identify ways children can exhibit friendliness.

Sermon: Ask: "How many of you have ever felt lonely? Did you feel better when someone spoke to you? Do you like for people to speak to you? When someone meets you, smiles, and says hello is that person friendly? When you say hello to others are you being friendly?

"Listen to the story and tell me whether or not Jesus was friendly."

Jesus and his disciples had walked all morning. They were on their way from Judea to the north country of Galilee. Jesus had chosen to travel the short route that went through Samaria. Jews never went that way if they could help it because they did not like the Samaritans.

It was noontime. The sun shown brightly. The weather was

hot when they finally came to a well near the village of Sychar.

Weary from travel, Jesus sat down beside the well to rest. His disciples left him there and went into the village to buy food.

Soon a Samaritan woman came to draw water from the well. Friendly Jesus spoke to her. "Give me a drink of water," he said.

The Samaritan woman was surprised. Why did he speak to me? she probably thought. I am a despised Samaritan and a woman. The Jews have no dealings with Samaritans. No Jewish man should speak to me.

Astonished she said to Jesus. "How is it that you being a Jew ask me a Samaritan woman for a drink?"

"If only you knew who I am and what God could give you," Jesus kindly replied, "you would ask me for a drink and I would give you living water."

"But sir," the confused Samaritan woman said. "How could you get the water? You have no rope and no draw bucket and the well is deep. Are you greater than our ancestor Jacob? He dug the well. He and his sons and his cattle drank of its water."

Respectfully Jesus explained that all who drink from the well would become thirsty again. But whoever drank of the water he gave would never thirst again.

Excitedly, the woman responded: "Please sir, give me some of that water. I will never be thirsty again. And I will not have to make this long trip out here everyday and draw water."

Jesus and the woman talked until the disciples returned. She then left her water jar at the well and ran back into the village.

"Come with me, please come with me and see a man who knows everything. Surely he is the Christ," she exclaimed to all she met.

The villagers listened to her and went out to the well to see Jesus.

Response: Ask: "Was Jesus friendly? How?

"I will suggest five ways to be friendly. If you agree with me, after each statement, raise your hand.

"I can be friendly by speaking to others.

"I can be friendly by listening when others talk.

"I can be friendly by answering questions kindly.

"I can be friendly by being kind to those who have few or no friends.

"I can be friendly by speaking first rather than waiting to be spoken to."

Prayer: God, help each of us to be friendly like Jesus was friendly, in whose name we pray, amen.

11
Jesus Was Forgiving

Preparation: Study Luke 23:20-49.

Sermon: Ask: "Has anyone ever made fun of you? Has anyone ever mistreated you? Did anyone tell something about you that was not true? How did it make you feel? (Give adequate time for response.)

"Jesus experienced some unkind things. Listen to find out what happened to him and what he did about it."

Pilate, looking at the crowd, asked, "What shall I do with Jesus who is called Christ?" The crowd shouted: "Let him be crucified! Crucify him! Crucify him!"

Although he had tried, Pilate realized that he could do nothing to change their minds. He gave Jesus to his soldiers who took him into a great hall before a large crowd of soldiers. They put a scarlet robe on Jesus and made a crown from long thorns and put it on his head. They put a stick in his right hand and pretended that it was a scepter. Then the soldiers made fun of Jesus. They knelt before him and shouted "Hail the King of the Jews." They spat on him and took the stick and beat him on the head.

Finally they put Jesus' own robe back on him and placed the cross on his shoulders and led him away to be crucified. While on their way to Golgotha, they came upon a man from Africa. Simon was his name. They forced him to carry the cross for Jesus.

Reaching Golgotha, they crucified Jesus along with two other men who were thieves.

The center cross held a sign which read, "This is Jesus, the King of the Jews."

At the foot of his cross, soldiers divided Jesus' clothing. They gambled to see which part of his garment each would get.

The priests who were responsible for Jesus' crucifixion stood watching. "He can save others! Let him save himself! Come down off the cross!" they jeered.

One of the thieves joined the mocking. "If you are really the Christ why don't you save yourself and us too?"

Through all the pain and through all the mockery, Jesus prayed. "Father," he said, "forgive these people. They do not know what they are doing."

Response: Ask: "Did Jesus try to get even with those who did him wrong? What did he do? How can we be like Jesus when someone wrongs us?"

Prayer: God, forgiving is hard to do. Show us how to forgive as Jesus forgave. In his name we pray, amen.

Bible

12
The Bible Is About God

Preparation: Secure a copy of a modern biography.

Sermon: Show the children the biography. Explain what kind of book you hold and tell a little about the person about whom the book is written. Say: "The Bible is a biography. Listen to the story that I will tell you and tell me whose biography the Bible is."

God made man and gave him a beautiful garden as his home. He made a woman to be the man's wife. He told the man and woman to care for the garden, and he made them rulers over all the animals.

God himself was a good friend to Adam and Eve, the first man and woman. They loved him and enjoyed being with him.

God told Adam and Eve that they could eat almost anything that grew in their garden home. However he pointed out one tree and said, "Do not eat the fruit from that tree. If you do, you will be punished."

One day Satan, God's enemy, talked to Eve about the tree from which they were not to eat. Satan wanted Adam and Eve to obey him rather than to obey God.

"Go ahead and eat some of the fruit," Satan said to Eve. He

made her see how pretty it was. He told her that nothing bad would happen if she disobeyed God.

Eve listened to Satan and ate some the forbidden fruit. So did Adam.

For the first time, a man and woman had chosen to do what they wanted to do instead of what God said for them to do. They discovered that disobeying God made them ashamed. They hid from God!

But God knew all about the people he had created. He knew that they had disobeyed him. "You have sinned," God told Adam and Eve. "Now you must be punished."

Adam and Eve had to leave their beautiful garden. No longer could they enjoy the perfect happiness and fellowship with God they had had at first. They had to work hard to get the food and clothing and shelter they needed.

God was sorry that the man and woman had sinned. But even as he had made them leave the garden, he proved that he still loved them. "Satan is the one who persuaded you to do wrong," God said. "One day I will send someone who will crush Satan and put an end to his ability to make trouble."

All the rest of the Bible is a history of how God kept his promise. The stories of Bible people show that God kept working to help them, kept loving them no matter how much they disobeyed him. When Jesus came to earth, God's promise came true. Jesus' life, death, and resurrection crushed the power of Satan. Through him any man can have forgiveness for his sins and power to make right choices. "The Father sent the Son to be the Saviour of the world" (1 John 4:14).

Response: Ask, "The Bible is the biography of whom? Name one thing the Bible tells us about God."

Prayer: Thank you, God, for the special biographical book that tells us about God and his great plan of sending his Son to the earth to show his love for every man. In whose name we pray, amen.

13
What Is the Bible?

Preparation: Prepare a series of the flash cards using the following terms—*God, book, 66, Old Testament, New Testament, 39, 27, Hebrew, Greek, about 40 men, 1,500 years,* and *many places.*

Sermon: Tell the children that you have prepared flash cards. Each flash card has printed on it information that tells one special fact about the Bible. Tell the group that you will show each of the flash cards and explain what fact that flash card tells about the Bible. Ask them to listen very carefully because you will ask them some questions about the Bible when you finish your story.

Many, many years ago, people did not know how to write. Since they could not write, there were no books. But there was God, and God did things for those people just as he does for us today.

Even though man could not write, he could talk. A family sat around the fire at night, and the father told stories about God. The children listened very carefully. Then when they had children of their own, they told the things they had learned about God from their fathers. They added stories of what God had done for them.

At last, man began to learn ways to write. Then it was possible for the stories about God to be written down and that is what the Bible is. (Hold up a flash card which says *God.*) The Bible is a book about God and what he has done for man since the very beginning.

The word *Bible* is interesting. It means *book*. (Hold up a flash card that says *book.*) When you talk about the Bible, you are really talking about the book.

The Bible is more than a book. It is a library, because inside the Bible there are many books. (Hold up the card that says *66.*) In fact, there are sixty-six books that make up the Bible.

The Bible is divided into two big sections. One section is the Old Testament. The other is the New Testament.

(Hold up a flash card which says *Old Testament.*) The Old Testament is larger than the New Testament. It was written before Jesus came to live on earth. If you look through your Bible starting at the front, you will come to the Old Testament first. It comes before the New Testament section.

(Hold up a flash card that says *New Testament.*) The second big part of the Bible is the New Testament. The New Testament does not have as many books as the Old. The New Testament is the part of the Bible that tells about Jesus and the people who loved him. The New Testament was written in the first hundred years after Jesus went back to heaven.

(Hold up the card which says *39.*) The Old Testament has thirty-nine books. The first book is Genesis. It tells about the beginning of things. The last book in the Old Testament is Malachi.

(Hold up the card that says *27.*) There are twenty-seven books in the New Testament. The first four of these are called the Gospels. They tell about the life of Jesus. Matthew, Mark, Luke, and John wrote the Gospels. Most of the other books in the New Testament are letters written by church leaders to churches and Christians.

(Hold up a flash card that says *Hebrew.*) The Bible was not written in English. It was written in two languages. The Old

Testament was written in the language called Hebrew. It was the language of the people of the Old Testament.

(Hold up the card that says *Greek.*) The New Testament was written in the Greek language. Greek was the language spoken in most parts of the world when the New Testament was being written.

(Hold up a card that says *about 40 men.*) Most books you read were written by one person. The Bible was written by about forty people. Some were shepherds who cared for sheep. Some were farmers. Others were fishermen. Some were kings who ruled nations while others were peasants who were very poor people.

All these people wrote because they knew God wanted them to give a message to people. The writers did not realize that what they wrote would become part of the book called the Bible. They did know that they were writing down a message that God wanted others to hear and know.

(Hold up a card that says *1,500 years.*) It took a long, long time for the Bible to be written. From the time the first part of the Bible was written until the last book was written was about 1,500 years. No wonder it took so many people to write the Bible. Nobody lives 1,500 years!

(Show the card that says *many places.*) Just as the Bible was written by many people through many years, it was written in many different places. Some of the Bible was written in the land where Jesus lived, the land of Palestine. Other parts of it were written where Daniel lived in the country of Babylon. Some of the Bible was written from a prison cell in Rome.

Response: Show the flash cards to the children and ask them to share a fact about the Bible of which the flash card reminds them.

Prayer: Thank you, God, for giving to us such a very special book, the Bible. In Jesus' name, amen.

14
God's Word Is a Guidebook

Preparation: Study Exodus 19.
Get a poster of a traffic signal light.

Sermon: Show the traffic signal poster to the children. Ask them to tell you what law is to be obeyed when the red light comes on—the green light—and the yellow light. Emphasize that laws have been made so that we can safely use the highways.

Ask: "Do you have laws at home to obey? Do you have rules at school to obey? Are there church rules to obey?

"I will tell you a story about a time when God gave us some very special laws. He knows that we will be happy if we will obey the laws that he has given to us.

"Listen to the story and discover what those laws are."

Three months had passed since the Hebrews left Egypt. Moses, their leader, had led them to a mountain called Sinai. He told them to set up their tents in the fields that were in front of the mountain.

God spoke to Moses and told him to climb up the mountain. God had a special message for Moses to give to the people. (Read Ex. 19:5.)

After God and Moses had finished talking, Moses came down out of the mountain and called the people together. He told them what God had said. The people said to Moses, "We will do all that God wants us to do."

Moses told the people that God would speak to them from the mountain and tell them what he wanted them to do. But first they must get ready.

So, for three days, the people cleaned their tents, washed their clothes, and took baths. After everything and everybody was clean, the people were ready to listen to God as he spoke to them from Sinai. Moses told the people to gather close to the mountain.

With those instructions, Moses went up into the mountain.

Soon the earth began to tremble, the people heard sounds of trumpets, and fire covered the mountain. Then a voice began to speak. It was the voice of God.

When the people heard God speaking, they became very much afraid.

God told them what he wanted them to do. We call the laws he gave them the Ten Commandments. Here are the laws God gave his people that day.

(Read from the Bible the Ten Commandments.)

Moses remembered all the instructions God gave. Later, he wrote them on a scroll. The Hebrew people called it the book of the Law. It was the part of our Bible that is in the first five books of the Old Testament.

Response: Say, "God wants us to obey those special rules today. He knows that if we will obey the rules that we will be happy."

Ask: "Are you happier when you obey your parents? Do you enjoy someone telling something about you that is not true? Do you like for people to steal what you have?

"God knows what will make us happy. Isn't God good?"

Prayer: Sing "God Is So Good."

15
God's Word Is Eternal

Preparation: Read Jeremiah 36.
Secure a penknife or pocketknife.

44/A Year of Children's Sermons

Sermon: Show the knife to the children. Say: "I hold in my hand a knife. A knife is a very important tool. The proper use of a knife helps one do many things. What is a knife used for?

"We have a very exciting story today. It is about a king who thought that he could destroy with a knife something that was very important. Listen to discover what happened."

God spoke to Jeremiah one day. He said: "Jeremiah, I've talked with you many times. I have told you things to tell to the people. This you have done. Now, Jeremiah, I want you to write down all the things that I have said to you."

Jeremiah obeyed the wishes of God. He found himself a secretary (or scribe) whose name was Baruch. Jeremiah told Baruch the words he wanted him to write. Baruch wrote them upon a scroll.

The friends and neighbors of Jeremiah gathered in the Temple to pray.

When the scroll was finished, Jeremiah asked Baruch to take it to the Temple and read it to the people. This Branch did.

Micaiah was at the Temple. He heard Baruch read the scroll. He immediately went to the king's house. He went into a room that was called the secretary's chamber. Here some of the king's helpers, called princes, were sitting.

Micaiah told the princes what he had heard. The princes sent for Baruch and asked him to read to them the scroll.

When Baruch read them the scroll, the princes became very much afraid. They asked Baruch if they could read the scroll to the king. Baruch said they could. The princes must have thought that the king would get mad when he heard what Jeremiah had written, because they told Baruch to go hide and take Jeremiah with him.

The princes went to the palace of the king. It was winter. Close to the king was a hearth, or brazier. In it a fire was burning to keep the king warm.

The princes showed the scroll to the king.

"Read it to me," commanded the king.

But when King Jehoiakim heard the words on the scroll, he became very angry. So angry did he become that he took a knife and cut the scroll into pieces and burned it in the fire that blazed in the brazier.

King Jehoiakim thought that he had destroyed God's Word.

But God spoke again to Jeremiah. "Take another scroll and write again the message I have given you," God instructed his prophet.

Jeremiah did what God asked him to do. Baruch helped, as before.

Do you know how we know this story about Jeremiah's scroll? It is written in the Bible, in the book of Jeremiah in the Old Testament.

Response: Ask: "What did King Jehoiakim think that he would destroy?" Help the children understand that King Jehoiakim could destroy a scroll but he could not destroy the message of God. Help them think about how long God's Word has lasted and remember that God has said that it will never be destroyed.

Prayer: Thank you, God, for your Word. Thank you for the promise that your Word is eternal and that it will never pass away. In Jesus' name, amen.

16
God's Word Is Powerful

Preparation: Study the temptation of Jesus in the wilderness, Matthew 4:1-11.

Sermon: Ask: "Have you ever been tempted to do something wrong? Have you ever wished for something that could help you always choose the right things to do?

"Jesus knew the secret. Jesus never did anything that was wrong. He was perfect.

"Listen to the story to discover what Jesus did when he was tempted to do wrong."

After his baptism, Jesus went into the wilderness. It was a hot, dry region. Wild beasts roamed over the burned-out landscape.

Alone in the wilderness, Jesus thought and prayed. For days he pondered about how he would show God's love to people on earth. He prayed and thought so hard that he did not eat for forty days.

"If you are the Son of God, make these stones become bread," a voice said to him.

Jesus recognized the voice. It was Satan. And the stones on the ground looked much like small loaves of bread. How tempted Jesus must have been to use his power selfishly. Also, Jesus knew that the people expected the Messiah to provide them with bread from heaven.

Although Jesus was tempted to do as Satan had suggested, he answered with a verse from the book of Deuteronomy. "Man shall not live by bread alone. He lives by the words that God speaks to him," replied Jesus.

The Jewish people believed that the Messiah would appear in the Temple in an unusual way. So Satan took Jesus up on a high tower of the Temple in Jerusalem.

Satan said: "If you really are God's Son, why don't you jump off of this tower? The Scripture says that God will send angels to keep you from harm."

Jesus must have been tempted to get the people to follow him by jumping from the tower. However, he answered Satan again with another verse from the book of Deuteronomy. "Do not tempt the Lord your God," Jesus quoted.

Satan did not give up. Somehow he showed Jesus all the kingdoms of the world and the glory of them. Both knew that the Jewish people believed that the Messiah would make Israel the ruler over all other nations. "If you will fall down and worship me, I will give you all these glorious kingdoms," Satan said.

With a sharp command Jesus answered, "Leave me alone! God has said to worship and serve him only."

So Satan left Jesus at that time. Then God sent angels to care for Jesus.

Response: Ask: "Was Jesus tempted to do things that were wrong? How was he always able to choose the right things to do? (*He used the Scriptures.*)

"The psalmist David must have discovered that secret. He once wrote, 'Thy word have I hid in mine heart, that I might not sin against thee' (Ps. 119:11).

"One hides God's Word in his heart when he memorizes verses from the Bible and understand what the verses mean. Bible verses are so powerful that they can help us to choose the right rather than the wrong.

"I challenge you boys and girls to memorize as many Scripture verses as you possibly can."

Prayer: God, thank you for your word, the Bible. Help us hide it in our hearts and learn what it means. Keep us from sinning against thee. In Jesus' name, amen.

Church

17
The Church Tells About Jesus

Preparation: Read Acts 8:26-40.
Find a picture of a Sunday School teacher teaching a group of children.

Sermon: Show the picture to the children. Say, "Tell me about this picture."

Pick up some statements the children will make to explain the role of a Sunday School teacher is that of helping others to know and understand the Bible. Say: "Listen to the story today about a man who enjoyed helping people understand the Bible. This teacher had a very unusual class. After the story tell me what made the class so unusual."

"Philip," said an angel of the Lord. "Go over to the desert road that runs from Jerusalem down to Gaza."

Philip did as he had been instructed. When he arrived at the designated place, he looked down the road to see a chariot approaching. A man of importance rode in the chariot. He was from Ethiopia and was in charge of Queen Candace's treasure. He was returning to Ethiopia from having worshiped in the Temple at Jerusalem.

"Go and meet the chariot," the Holy Spirit said to Philip.

Philip ran toward the chariot. As he neared it, he heard the man from Ethiopia reading aloud from the book of the prophet Isaiah.

"Do you understand what you are reading?" Philip asked.

"No, I do not understand. How can I unless someone explains it to me? Please come and sit with me and instruct me in what the Scripture is saying," said the Ethiopian.

Philip got into the chariot, sat down, and began to tell the man about Jesus.

As they rode along, they came to a pond of water. "Look!" the Ethiopian exclaimed, "there is water. Why can I not be baptized?"

"You can be baptized," answered Philip, "if you believe with all your heart that which I have told you about Jesus."

Immediately the Ethiopian replied, "I believe that Jesus Christ is the Son of God."

The Ethiopian gave a command to stop the chariot. They got out of the chariot and walked into the water. Then Philip baptized him.

Philip was just one of many early church members who told others about Jesus. Philip was doing what Jesus had asked his friends to do when he said, "Everywhere you go, tell others about me."

Telling others about Jesus is the most important work that the church does.

Response: Ask: "Who was the teacher? Did he have an unusual class? How many were in the class? Where did the class meet?

"Teachers today tell others about Jesus just as Philip did long ago."

Use the remaining time to share ways your church teaches the gospel. Describe places where the gospel is taught.

50/A Year of Children's Sermons

Prayer: Thank you, God, for asking us to tell others about Jesus. Thank you for letting us tell the good news. In Jesus' name, amen.

18
The Church Prays Together

Preparation: Read Acts 12:1-19.
Seriously rethink your belief about the power of prayer.
Find a picture of someone praying.

Sermon: Show a picture of someone praying. Ask: "What is the person in the picture doing? What is prayer? Why does one pray? Do you ever pray 'thank you' prayers? What have you thanked God for? Do you ever ask God for something when you pray? What have you asked God for? Do you ever pray for someone?

"Our story today is about a time when the church gathered to pray for someone. Listen for the reason the people prayed, who they prayed for, and the results of their prayers."

"Come to my house," said Mary, the mother of John Mark. "We can pray there and no one will bother us."

Soon the friends of Jesus crowded into her house. They began to pray for their friend Simon Peter. King Herod had put Peter into prison. The king was waiting for the night to pass which would end the Passover celebration. Then he would have Peter tried and probably condemned to death. King Herod had already killed James, the brother of John.

The night was quickly passing. Soon daylight would come. As the moments ticked away, the church people prayed for Peter's safety.

Meanwhile in the prison, Peter was chained to two soldiers. Although knowing that with the coming of day he would probably face death, Peter was able to lay down and sleep.

During the night, someone gently shook him. "Wake up, Peter! Get up and get dressed. Put your shoes and coat on and come with me."

Peter obeyed. He arose, dressed, and followed the strange person. They passed the guards but no one tried to stop them. They came to the iron gate that led into the street. It opened on its own accord.

Out into the street they went. The stranger, who was an angel from God, walked with Peter for one block. Then he disappeared.

All this time Peter thought he was dreaming. Suddenly it dawned upon him that the things were real that were happening to him. He really was free. He really was out of prison.

Quickly he went to Mary's house. The church people could hardly believe their eyes when they saw Peter. Joyfully Peter told about the angel that God sent who led him from the prison.

"You must tell the other church friends," Peter said. "Tell them about how wonderfully God has answered your prayers."

Response: Ask: "Why did the people pray? For whom did they pray? What happened?"

Conclude by sharing a recent result from prayers of the church.

Prayer: Thank you, God, for the power you give us through prayer. In Jesus' name, amen.

19
The Church Has Leaders

Preparation: Read Acts 6:1-8.

Invite a church helper to sit with you when you present the following sermon.

Sermon: Introduce the church helper who is sitting with you. Ask the helper a few questions about how he helps the church. Provide opportunity for the children to ask some questions should they wish to do so.

Say, "Today I will tell you a story about the time when the church elected its first helpers. Find out why the church needed helpers and what the helpers did."

"We are not being treated fairly," complained the widows who spoke Greek. "Each day the Hebrew widows get more food than we do. We are being overlooked and neglected."

Some of the members of the early church did not have anywhere to live. Others had no money for food. There were those who lost their jobs when they became friends with Jesus. Church members who had food and money shared them. They gave it to the apostles to divide with the poor and needy church members. That made the apostles have too much to do. They were already busy as could be with teaching and preaching about Jesus, healing the sick, and taking care of the poor.

The apostles talked about the problem. "We have too much to do," they said. "Our most important job is to teach and preach about Jesus. Making sure that everyone has enough food to eat takes lots of time. We should do nothing that will take away our time from preaching and teaching. Let's ask the church to choose some men to help us."

So the twelve apostles called the church together for a business meeting. The apostles explained the problem. Then they said, "Look around you. Choose seven men who are wise, who are well thought of by everyone, and who are full of the Holy Spirit. We will put them in charge of feeding the poor.

"Then we can use our time to pray, preach, and teach."

The church members thought the apostles had a good plan. They did as the apostles suggested and selected seven men to be church helpers.

After the church members made their selection, the apostles led the church in a special service. The apostles laid their hands on the heads of the seven men and prayed a special prayer for them.

Response: Ask: "Why were church helpers needed? What did they do? Do you know what those first helpers are now called? (*Deacons.*)

"Let me introduce you to some of our church helpers."

Use the remaining time to introduce groups of workers such as deacons, Sunday School teachers, and so forth.

Prayer: Thank you, God, for our church and for the many people who help our church do the good things it does. In Jesus' name, amen.

20
What Is the Church?

Preparation: Study Acts 2.
Get a model of a church building or a teaching picture of one.

54/A Year of Children's Sermons

Sermon: Show the church building to the children. Ask, "What do I hold in my hand?"

The response most likely will be, "a church."

Say: "I will tell you a story about a church. Listen and tell me whether or not the church in the story is a building."

Jesus took his friends to Mount Olivet and talked with them. He told them that he wanted them to tell everyone they knew about him. But he said that they were not to start telling about him just yet. They were to go back into Jerusalem and wait until they received the power to tell others about him.

The friends of Jesus returned to Jerusalem and did just what Jesus told them to do.

They gathered together in an upstairs room. While they waited to receive the power of which Jesus spoke, they chose a man to take the place of Judas, the disciple who had betrayed Jesus. Matthias was selected.

On the day that the feast of Pentecost was to be celebrated, the power for which they were waiting came.

"Listen," someone must have said. A sound like a strong, violent wind filled the house. And brightness like a tongue of fire appeared and glowed above the head of each person in the room. The Bible says that the Holy Spirit came. When the Holy Spirit came, the friends of Jesus received the power they needed to tell others about Jesus.

In Jerusalem, at that time, were Jewish people from all over the world. They spoke languages that the Jews living in Jerusalem could not understand. However, the friends of Jesus were able to talk to those foreign Jews in the languages that the foreign Jews spoke! They had received the power to tell others of Jesus.

"How can this be?" some of the people questioned. "How can these men from Galilee speak our language?"

Others in the crowd made fun of the friends of Jesus. "These

Church/55

men are drunk," they said. "They have found some new wine."

Soon Simon Peter, the fisherman, stood to speak. What a sermon he preached that day! The power that Peter had received gave him the ability to tell about Jesus in a most convincing way. In fact, the sermon was so powerful that three thousand people believed what Peter preached about Jesus.

These friends of Jesus did many things together.

The friends of Jesus were students. The Bible said they studied the teachings of Jesus.

They liked each other. They liked to be together.

They took the Lord's Supper together.

They prayed together.

They shared. The Bible tells us that they sold what they owned and shared the money with each other.

They ate together.

They were happy. They praised God.

Response: Ask: "Was the church a building? Was the church a group of people? What things did the people do?

"Boys and girls, the building we meet in today is not the church. The building cannot tell about Jesus, can it? The building cannot pray, can it? The building cannot share, can it?

"Who tells about Jesus? Who prays? Who shares? You are right. The people who come together in this building do those things.

"Remember, even though we sometimes call this building the church, the church is really the people who gather here to worship God."

Prayer: Thank you, God, for the church. Thank you for giving the church the power it needs to tell about Jesus. In his name we pray, amen.

21
The Church Helps People

Preparation: Read Acts 11:19-30.
Have money ready to show the children.

Sermon: Ask: "How many of you ever needed help and someone gave you the help that you needed?

"Do you know that the church helps people who need help?"

Show the money. Say: "Today, you will hear a story about how a church helped some people. Listen to discover how the church used money to help friends in need."

Many Christians lived in the city of Antioch. These Christians banded together and formed a church. They told the good news about Jesus to everyone that would listen—Jews, Greeks, and Romans.

News about the Antioch church reached the church in Jerusalem. The Jerusalem church leaders wanted to know more about the things that were happening in Antioch.

"Let's send Barnabas to Antioch. He is a good man and a faithful worker. Whatever he reports, we can believe," said the Jerusalem church leaders.

Barnabas traveled from Jerusalem to Antioch. There he found some wonderful things happening. They were so wonderful that he decided to stay in Antioch and help the church members.

Barnabas soon discovered there was so much to do that he needed help.

Barnabas probably remembered the time in Jerusalem when he befriended Saul, the once persecutor of Christians. He would be a good helper, thought Barnabas. Soon Barnabas was on his way to Tarsus. He would find Saul and try to persuade him to help with the Antioch church.

Barnabas found Saul and told Saul about the many exciting things that were happening in the Antioch church. Saul agreed to go with Barnabas and help.

For an entire year, Barnabas and Saul worked together. They enjoyed many wonderful experiences.

In Antioch, the followers of Christ were given a nickname. People began calling them Christians.

One day the Antioch church received some visitors. They were prophets who came from Jerusalem.

One of them was named Agabus. As he spoke to the Antioch church, he said: "Soon, a great famine will come upon the land of Israel. Your friends in Jerusalem will need money to buy food."

"Let's help our Jerusalem friends," said the church members in Antioch. "Each of us will give as much money as we can. We will send the money to our Jerusalem friends. Then when the famine comes, they can use the money to buy food."

So the Antioch church collected an offering and sent it to the church leaders in Jerusalem by Barnabas and Saul.

Response: Ask: "Did the Antioch church help the church in Jerusalem? How?

"Boys and girls, I want to share with you some ways our church helps people."

Use the remaining time in relating some of the benevolent ministries of your church.

Prayer: Thank you, God, for churches that help people who have needs. Thank you for our church and for the many things it does to help people. In Jesus' name, amen.

Self

22
I Can Become

Preparation: Read Genesis 37:1-11; 42-44.

Sermon: Tell the children about a dream that you may have had as a child. Ask: "Do you ever dream? Do you ever tell your dreams to anyone? Have any of your dreams come true?

"The Bible tells about a young man who dreamed. Listen to find out who dreamed and if his dreams came true."

"I had a strange dream," Joseph said to his brothers. "I dreamed that we were out in the field cutting and binding wheat. Suddenly my shock of wheat stood up straight, but your shocks all bowed down to mine."

"What are you saying, Joseph?" the brothers retorted. "Do you think that you will become our boss and that we will bow before you? Do you really believe that someday you will reign over us?"

Joseph's brothers did not like him. They had their reasons. Jacob, their father, loved Joseph better than he did any of the other boys. And Jacob showed his favoritism when he gave Joseph a very special coat. Furthermore, Joseph was a tattler. Whenever he worked with his brothers in the field, he would return home to tell on them. So, his dreaming made his brothers hate Joseph more than ever.

Later, Joseph had another dream. He dreamed that the sun, the moon, and eleven stars bowed to him.

Can you imagine how that dream caused Joseph's brothers to feel toward him?

Jacob heard Joseph telling about his second dream. "Really, Joseph," his father said, "do you honestly believe that someday your brothers and I will bow on the earth before you?"

Years passed. A terrible famine came upon the land. Food became scarce.

Learning of grain in Egypt, Jacob sent his sons there to buy food.

The shepherds finally stood before the governor of Egypt, bowed respectfully, and asked for grain.

It just so happened that the governor turned out to be Joseph whom the brothers had sold to Midianite traders several years before.

Yes! As a young boy, Joseph dreamed of what he would someday become. That dream came true.

Response: Ask: "Who dreamed? Did his dreams come true?

"Boys and girls, what kind of person do you want to become? Joseph dreamed about what he wanted to become. And finally his dream came true. So it is with you. You will become the kind of person you dream about becoming.

"A verse in the Bible says something like this. 'Whatever a person thinks he is that is what he becomes.' What do you dream of becoming?"

Prayer: God, give each of us dreams about ourselves. Help each of us to dream about becoming like Jesus. Help us each day to become more like him. In his name we pray, amen.

23
I Am Special

Preparation: Read the creation story from Genesis 1—2. Read it from the perspective of the greatness of man.

Find some object that you created that is very special to you.

Sermon: Show the children your creation. Tell what it is, how it came into existence, and why it is so special to you. Say, "I will tell you a story about a person who made many things. Of all the things he made he chose one as his very special creation. Listen to discover who it was that created, and what he created that was so very special."

Away back as far as one can go back—to the very beginning—God was there.

God spoke. "Let there be light," he said. And light appeared.

God looked at the light he had made and saw that it was good. The light he called day. And the darkness he called night.

Again, God spoke. This time, he said, "Let there be an atmosphere, a sky for the world I am making." The voice of God was obeyed and an atmosphere was formed.

God spoke a third time. He said, "Let the waters pond into seas and oceans, and let dry land appear upon the earth." Again, the voice of God was obeyed.

When God spoke again, grass began to grow on the earth as did herbs and fruit trees.

About that which he had spoken into existence, God said, "That's good."

God spoke the fourth time and created the sun, moon, and stars. That too pleased him and again he said, "That's good."

No birds flew in the air. No animals roamed upon the earth and no fish swam in the sea until God spoke again. God looked at the birds. He looked at the fish. He looked at the animals. Then he said, "That's good."

Thus far, God had made everything through speaking a command.

Now all was ready for God's very best creation.

God spoke once more. "Let us make man," he said. "Let us make man to be like us. And let him be the boss over everything that we have made."

Because man was special, and the very best thing God was to create, God did not speak or command man into existence. Rather, God worked with the dust of the ground he had made. Much like a potter who molds pots from clay, God formed an object that looked like a person's body. But the body could not walk and talk or cry or laugh. Then God did something very special. He breathed into that clay body, and the Bible says man became a living soul.

Response: Ask: "Who was the creator? What was his very best creation?

"Boys and girls, God made you. You too are one of the very best things God has ever made. Because you are a part of his best, God thinks of you as being very, very special.

Prayer: Thank you, God, for making us so very, very special. Help us to always remember how special we are. In Jesus' name, amen.

24
I Have Abilities

Preparation: Study Matthew 25:14-30.

Find pictures that illustrate people using their abilities. Select pictures that show people using homemaking skills and manual labor abilities as well as the talents of the arts.

Sermon: Show the pictures one at a time to the children. Ask them to tell you what ability the person in the picture is using. Lend assistance where needed.

Say: "Jesus told a story about three men who had abilities. Listen to discover how those men used their abilities."

"I plan to go on a long journey," a master said to three of his servants. "You must take care for my business while I am gone."

To one servant, the master gave five talents or five large sums of money. To another servant the master gave two talents and to the third servant, the master gave one talent. Immediately, the master left on his journey.

The servant who received the five talents had the ability to put the money to use and make five other talents. That he did.

Also, the servant who received the two talents had the ability to put his master's money to use and to make two other talents. That he did.

Now the third servant who received the one talent also had the ability to put his master's money to use. However, he was different from the first two in that he was afraid to use the money. Instead he dug a hole in the ground and there hid his master's money.

A long time passed but finally the master returned.

"Tell me about how well you used my money while I was gone," the master said to the three servants.

The first one to speak was the man who had received the five talents. "My lord," he said, "you gave to me five talents. I put your money to use and have doubled the amount you gave to me."

"Excellent!" responded the master. "You are a good servant because you have done well with a little. I will put you in charge of much."

The second servant who had also doubled the amount of his master's money received the same praise as did the first servant.

But the third servant dug up the money and brought to his master the same amount the master had given him. "Sir," the servant said, "I was afraid to use your money, so I dug a hole and hid it. Here it is."

"You are a terrible and lazy servant," thundered the master. "You should have taken my money and have put it to use.

"Take away the money from him and give it to the servant who had the ten talents."

Response: Ask: "Did each one receive some money? Did each receive the same amount of money? Why not? (*Each was given according to his ability.*)

"Why was the master pleased with two of his servants? Why was he displeased with the third one?

"Boys and girls, God has given to each of you special abilities. Each of you can do at least one thing well. You must discover your ability and then use that ability every time you can and as best you can."

Prayer: God, help each of us discover the ability you have given to us. Help us use that ability as best we can. Help us be a person of whom you will be proud. In Jesus' name, amen.

25
I Can Improve

Preparation: Study Luke 9:51-56 and the letters of John. Secure a broken toy.

Sermon: Show the children the broken toy. Ask: "Is there something wrong with this toy? What is wrong with it? Can this toy be improved? How? What do you do when you improve something?

"I want to tell you a story about a man that Jesus knew. Listen to decide if you think this friend of Jesus improved."

Jesus and his disciples were on their way to Jerusalem. Passing through Samaria, Jesus sent messengers ahead. "Reserve rooms for us in the Samaritan village," he requested. Reaching the village the messengers set about to do as they had been instructed. Though they tried hard, they could not reserve a room. The Samaritans hated the Jews and refused to let Jews stay in their village.

Word soon reached Jesus. "No room is reserved because the Samaritans refused to oblige."

James and John, who were brothers, became very much upset over the incident. In fact, they grew so angry with the Samaritans that they wanted to destroy them. "Master," they said, "remember Elijah called fire down from heaven that destroyed parts of an army. Would you wish us to command fire to come from heaven and burn up the Samaritans?"

Such attitudes displeased Jesus very much. He turned to James and John and spoke quite sharply to them for suggesting such action.

James and John were so outspoken and quick-tempered that Jesus nicknamed them the "Sons of Thunder."

Many years passed. John became an old man. Taking his pen

in hand he wrote letters to his friends. "My little children," he wrote, "love one another."

Could that be the same John who only a few years before wanted to call fire down from heaven upon the Samaritans? Yes, it was John, the brother of James. But he was different. He had improved. He had discovered how to replace hate with love because he had learned from Jesus.

Response: Ask: "Did John ever need to improve? Did he improve? How? Do you always do right? Are there times when you need to improve?

"Boys and girls, like John, you can improve. Isn't it good to know that even though we should do wrong today we can improve and do better tomorrow? I am glad that God helps us improve, aren't you? Let's thank him for it."

Prayer: Thank you, God, for the story about John. Thank you for making us so that we can improve even though we do wrong. Help each of us this week to improve in some area of our life. In Jesus' name, amen.

Friends

26
Friends Depend on Each Other

Preparation: Read Matthew 4:18-22; 9:9-13; 28:16-20.

Purchase a small carton of milk. Think about the many people that were involved in the production of that milk.

Sermon: Show the children the carton of milk. Ask, "Do I have to depend upon anyone to get this milk?" Review with the children the many people involved in the production of milk—farmers, truck drivers, people at the milk processing plants, the milkman, and the groceryman.

Say: "In most everything we do, we must depend on others to help us. That is one reason why friends are so important. We can depend on our friends to help us. Jesus did. Listen to the story and learn how Jesus depended on his friends to help him do his work. Listen to learn whether or not Jesus depends on his friends today to help do his work."

Jesus was ready to start his work. He needed some friends to help him. He did not wish to work alone.

One day he walked along the beach of the Sea of Galilee. He saw two men, Simon who was also called Peter and Andrew his brother. They were throwing a fishing net into the sea for they were fishermen by trade.

"Peter, Andrew," Jesus called. "Come with me. Let me be your guide, and I will make you fishers of men." Without hesitation, Peter and Andrew dropped their fishing nets and went with Jesus.

On up the beach they saw more fishermen. Zebedee and his two sons, James and John, sat in a boat mending their fishing nets. Jesus spoke to James and John much the same way he had spoken to Simon Peter and Andrew. "Come and follow me," he called. The response to the call was exactly as before. James and John got out of the boat, left their father Zebedee, and followed Jesus.

Near Capernaum, Jesus saw a publican—a man who collected taxes. "Come and be my disciple," Jesus said to Matthew. Immediately Matthew jumped up from his tax collecting booth and went with Jesus.

Similar experiences took place until Jesus had chosen twelve men to be his very special helpers.

When Jesus finished his work here on earth, he called his friends together. They walked to a place called Olivet. Jesus would soon go back to be with his Father in heaven. He had a special job for his friends to do. He must depend on them to carry on the work that he had started. He said to his friends: "Go everywhere. Preach the good news about me. Teach people to do what I have taught you. Baptize in the name of the Father, the Son, and the Holy Spirit those who believe your message."

Having spoken those words, Jesus left his friends and returned to his Father.

Response: Ask: "Did Jesus depend on his friends for help? Does Jesus depend on his friends today? Why? How can you be a friend to Jesus?"

Prayer: Thank you, God, for letting us be a friend to Jesus. May we always be the kind of persons Jesus can depend on to help him do his work. In Jesus' name, amen.

27
Friends Help Each Other

Preparation: Read Mark 2:1-12.
Find pictures of children doing helpful deeds.

Sermon: Say, "Do you sometimes sing a song that goes like this?

> Friends! Friends! Friends!
> I have some friends I love!
> I love my friends and they love me,
> I help my friends and they help me;
> Friends! Friends! Friends!
> I have some friends I love!
> ELIZABETH McE. SHIELDS

"Look at these pictures. Tell me how these boys and girls are being helpful."

Show the pictures and give the children ample time to respond.

Say, "Listen to the story to discover how these friends helped each other."

"Jesus is in town! Jesus is in town!" The news spread quickly through the streets of Capernaum. People became excited, especially those who had sick friends and sick family members.

"Where is Jesus?" the people asked.

Soon the people discovered the place where Jesus was staying. Quickly the house filled with people. After awhile there was no more room. Not another person could get in the house. People crowded through the doors and out into the yard.

Five friends lived in Capernaum. Four of them could walk, but one could not. He was paralyzed.

"We must get our sick friend to Jesus," said the four friends. "Jesus can make him well."

The four men made a pallet. They put their paralyzed friend on the pallet. Then each of the friends picked up a corner of the pallet and started toward the house where Jesus was.

When they came to the house, they saw the crowd. They could not get near the house. And besides, the doors were blocked with people.

We must get our friend to Jesus, thought the four friends. What can we do?

"Why not go up the outside stairs to the flat roof? We can tear away enough roof tiles to make space for our friend and his bed to go through. Then we will lower him on his bed into the house," suggested one friend.

The other three thought that the idea was a good one. So upon the roof they climbed. They tore away roof tiles until they had a hole large enough for the man and his bed to be lowered through.

Slowly, so very slowly, they lowered their sick friend until he lay on the floor in front of Jesus.

Jesus knew that the sick man's friends had faith that he could heal their friend.

He said to the man sick of palsy: "Thy sins be forgiven thee. Arise, take up thy bed and go thy way into thy house."

Receiving those instructions, the sick man did as Jesus commanded. He was no longer paralyzed. He could really walk!

Response: Ask, "Why did the friends help each other?"

Think of one way you can help a friend of yours this week. (Give a few volunteers the opportunity to share how they plan to help a friend.)

Prayer: Thank you, God, for helpful friends. In Jesus' name, amen.

28
Friends Rejoice Together

Preparation: Study Luke 1.

Sermon: Say: "Think of something good that happened to you last week. Did you tell anyone about it? If you told a friend, raise your hand.

"Our story is about some friends who had something good to happen to them. Listen to learn what the good thing was and with whom this thing was shared.

Zacharias busily burned incense. That was his job as a Temple priest. As the smoke from the incense floated upward, a huge crowd of people prayed.

The prayers ended. The crowd waited for Zacharias to come from the Temple. For a long time they waited. "Why is he staying so long?" they questioned. "Has something happened to him?"

When Zacharias finally appeared, he could not speak. He was speechless.

"He must have seen a vision," the crowd reasoned.

Back at home, his wife Elisabeth waited for Zacharias to return. What surprising news Zacharias would tell her.

For years Zacharias and Elisabeth had wished for children but had none. Now they thought they were too old to have a baby.

When Zacharias reached home, he wrote notes to Elisabeth. "The angel Gabriel visited me while I worked in the Temple and told me that we would become the parents of a baby boy. I did not believe him, and he said that I would not be able to speak until after our baby is born."

Shortly afterwards, Gabriel visited a young woman in Nazareth. "Mary," he said. "You are a very special person. God has chosen you to be the mother of Jesus. Your cousin Elisabeth is also expecting a baby."

I must share this good news with someone, Mary must have thought.

She soon left Nazareth and went to visit her cousin. When they saw each other, they rejoiced together over the good thing that would soon happen to each of them.

Sure enough, things happened as predicted. News of John's birth spread quickly. Relatives and friends gathered to rejoice with Zacharias and Elisabeth.

Response: Ask: "What good thing happened to Zacharias and Elisabeth? What good thing happened to Mary? Did they share their good news with friends? Did the good news make their friends happy?"

"Isn't God wonderful to give us friends with whom we can rejoice? Let's thank him for them."

Prayer: Dear God. Thank you for wonderful friends with whom we can share. In Jesus' name, amen.

29
Friends Love at All Times

Preparation: Study 1 Samuel 18:1-16; 19:1-10; 20.
Find a gift that a friend has given to you.

Sermon: Show the children the gift from a friend. Tell some of the circumstances that surrounded the giving of the gift. Talk about your friend and communicate how much his/her friendship means to you.

Say, "I am thinking of a Bible verse that says 'A friend loveth at all times.' Will you say that verse with me?"

"Our story is about two friends. Listen and discover whether or not these friends loved each other at all times."

"I love you very much," Jonathan said to his friend David. "To show you that you are my special friend, I will give you my belt, sword, bow, and coat. They are yours."

But Jonathan's father, King Saul, became jealous of David. Saul thought that the people of his kingdom liked David more than the king.

At times King Saul grew depressed and sad. When that happened, David, who was a good musician, played the harp and sang before the king.

One day as Saul sat listening to David, he held a spear in his hand. Suddenly he hurled the spear at David who jumped aside and then fled from the room.

"Arrest David! Kill him!" ordered the king.

When Jonathan heard what had happened, he hurried to his father. "My father," he said. "How has David wronged you? Did he not risk his life to fight Goliath?"

Saul agreed with his son. "David has nothing to fear. I will no longer seek his life," said Saul.

Happy times returned.

However, the happy times did not last long. The old sickness again possessed the king. Once more he tried to kill David.

This time David ran away. Saul ordered his army to search for David. Learning of the search, David went to see his good friend Jonathan.

"But I do not believe my father is trying to kill you," Jonathan argued. "Should not I, his son, be the first to know of such?" he asked.

The two friends worked out a plan to discover for sure whether or not Saul really plotted to kill David.

Much to his sorrow, Jonathan discovered that David was correct.

Tearfully and sadly Jonathan broke the news to David. "My father does seek your life," Jonathan said. "We have been friends from the time we met. Let's continue to be friends. Let's promise that as long as we live we will be kind to each other's families."

Response: Ask: "Who were the two friends? Did they love each other when things were good? Did they love each other when things were bad?

"Isn't it wonderful to have loving friends?"

"Boys and girls, God is our friend—our best friend. Remember he loves you at all times."

Prayer: Dear God. Thank you for being our very best friend. Thank you for loving us at all times. In Jesus' name, amen.

30
Friends Are Loyal and True

Preparation: Read 1 Samuel 24.

Sermon: Ask: "How many of you have some real good friends? What are the names of some of your friends? (Allow a few responses.) Have any of you thought that someone was a good friend only to find out that he was doing things to hurt you?

"Our story today is about a man who thought he had a good friend. Listen to find out what happens."

After David killed the giant Goliath, the people sang:
"Saul has killed his thousands, and David his ten thousands."
Hearing the song made King Saul extremely jealous. David will take my kingdom away from me, thought Saul. Even though David was one of Saul's best soldiers and a good friend of his son, Jonathan, Saul plotted to kill David.

David hid from Saul. Men who loved David began to follow him. Soon he had a small army.

News reached Saul that David and his men were out in the hill country. Saul took an army of three thousand men and started to search for David.

Along the way, they came to a big cave. Saul wanted to stop.

Unknown to King Saul, David and his small army were hiding back in the deep shadows of the cave.

"Now is your chance, David," his men whispered. "Saul is in your hands. You can do with him what you want to."

Very slowly and carefully, so as to not make a sound, David crept close to the king. He raised his sword. Very, very carefully, David lifted the king's robe and, without being caught, cut off the king's skirt. Quietly, David disappeared back into the darkness of the cave.

David's army was disappointed. "God chose Saul to be the king. And for that reason I must not harm him," David explained.

Saul left the cave. David followed him.

"My Lord the king!" David yelled.

The king turned to see David holding the piece of cloth he had cut from Saul's skirt.

Respectfully David explained to the king why his life was spared.

When David finished speaking, Saul said, "Is that your voice, my son David?" Then he wept. "You are a better man than I am. You have been good to me and I have tried to kill you. Someday you will be king. Promise me that you will not hurt my family."

David promised. Saul returned home. David and his men went back into the cave.

Response: Ask: "Was Saul a true friend to David? Was David a true friend to Saul? Which of the two does this song describe?

> A friend loveth at all times, When things are good or bad.
> A friend loveth at all times, Rejoiceth when we're glad.
> A friend helpeth in trouble, A friend is always true;
> A friend loveth at all times, A friend I'll be to you.°

What can we learn from David?"

Prayer: Dear God, you want us to live at peace with each other. Help us to learn from David not to try to get even with those who do us wrong. In Jesus' name, amen.

°Mildred Hammon. Copyright 1950, Broadman Press. All rights reserved.

31
Friends Are Friendly

Preparation: Read 2 Kings 4:8-17.

Sermon: Say, "I know a Bible verse that says, 'A man that hath friends must show himself friendly' (Prov. 18:24). In other words, if I want friends I must be friendly. Will you say the verse with me?

"Listen to the story to find out if the people in the story became friends because one of them was friendly."

Elisha was a prophet. He traveled a lot. Many times his travels took him through the town of Shunem.

As Elisha went through Shunem one day, a kind, wealthy lady said to him, "Come into my house and eat some bread." Elisha was glad to have an invitation for a meal. He accepted the kind offer from the friendly lady. That proved to be the beginning of a wonderful friendship. In fact, from then on, every time Elisha passed through Shunem he stopped at this lady's house and ate a meal.

"I believe that the man who so often passes through here is a holy man of God," the lady said to her husband. "Let's build a small room upon our roof for this man of God. We can put a bed, a table, a stool, and a candlestick in the room. When the good man comes through, he will have a room of his own."

Her husband agreed with the plan. Before long the room was ready.

The next time Elisha went to Shunem, he had a very pleasant surprise. He was happy to have a room of his very own.

"The kind lady has gone to a lot of trouble to make this room so attractive and comfortable," said Elisha. "I want to express my appreciation to her by doing something good for her. Could

I speak a good word about her to the king or to the commander of the army? What could I do?"

Gehazi, Elisha's servant said, "This fine lady has no son and her husband is old."

"Go call her," Elisha said.

The kind woman appeared and stood in the doorway. Elisha said: "You have been so kind to me. Because of your kindness, God will bless your home with a baby boy. This time next year, you will hold him in your arms."

"Do not tell me something that is not true," replied the lady. She could not believe such happy news.

Sure enough, the year passed. The following spring, the lady of Shunem became the mother of a baby boy, just as Elisha had said.

Response: How did the woman and her husband show friendliness to Elisha? How did Elisha show friendliness to the lady and her husband?

Ask: "How many of you like to have friends? How many of you remember what the Bible says about how to make friends? Who can say that Bible verse for me?

"Think with me. Let's think of ways to be friendly to your classmates and playmates. Think of as many ways as you can." (Allow sufficient time for response.)

Prayer: Dear God. Thank you for friends. Thank you for telling us how to make friends. Help us this week to be friendly to our classmates and playmates. In Jesus' name, amen.

Home and Family

32
Forgiving My Family

Preparation: Read Genesis 37; 43—45.

Sermon: Ask: "Do you find forgiving someone who does you wrong an easy thing to do? Is forgiving some member of your family easy to do?

"Today I want to tell you a story about how forgiveness made a difference in a family. Listen to discover what that difference was."

Eleven frightened brothers bowed respectfully when the governor of Egypt entered the room. They presented him presents they had brought from their home in faraway Canaan.

As Governor Joseph looked at the brothers, he most likely remembered some dreams that he had had many years before. He remembered that he had dreamed of being out in the field with his brothers cutting wheat. Suddenly his shock of wheat stood up straight. His brothers' shocks bowed to his. He remembered what his brothers said when he told them his dream. "Do you really think that you will be our boss someday?" they sneered. He remembered his second dream. The sun, moon and eleven stars bowed before him. The governor remembered the jealousy that his brothers displayed when he shared that dream with the

Home and Family/79

members of his family.

The governor's memory did not stop with the recall of his dreams. His mind wandered back to some weeks after his dreams. He remembered how upon his father's request he went to check about his brothers. How could he forget the welcome that his brothers gave him. They grabbed him, took off his coat that his father had given to him, and threw him into a dark empty pit.

Nor could the governor forget how those same brothers sold him to some Ishmaelite merchants who took him to Egypt and sold him as a slave.

Unbeknowing to his brothers, the governor of Egypt, before whom they stood, was the brother whom they had mistreated years before.

Now Governor Joseph had his chance. He had the power to get revenge! The brothers were at his mercy.

"Make everyone leave the room," Governor Joseph commanded.

Everyone left. Only the Governor and his brothers remained.

A strange thing happened. The governor of Egypt began to weep. He cried so loudly that those outside the room heard him. He turned to his brothers and said, "I am Joseph, your brother. Is my father still alive?"

Joseph's brothers could not speak. They were scared to be in the same room with him.

"Do not be afraid. Come near me. Do not be angry with yourselves or distressed because you sold me here. It was God who sent me here so I could save your lives."

What a joyful reunion took place that day. How happy Joseph's brothers were to know that Joseph had forgiven them.

Response: Ask: "Did forgiveness make a difference in Joseph's family? How?

"Do you think that forgiveness will make a difference in your family? Will your family be happier if you forgive those who mistreat you?"

Prayer: Dear God. Forgiving someone is very hard to do. Help us to be able to forgive those who wrong us, especially those in our family. In Jesus' name, amen.

33
Living Peaceably with My Family

Preparation: Read Genesis 13:6-18.
On a piece of poster board draw two faces, a smiling face and a frowning face.

Sermon: Point to the smiling face and ask, "Does your family ever look like this?"
Point to the frowning face and ask: "Does your family ever look like this? Does your family look like this when someone in the family fusses?

"The story that I will tell you begins with a family that looks like this. (Point to the smiling face.) Something happened that could have made the family look like this. (Point to the frowning face.)

"Listen to the story and discover which face best describes the family when the story ends."

Abram was a very rich man. He had lots of silver and gold and many cattle.
Lot was Abram's nephew. He too had many flocks and herds and tents.
Lot lived near his uncle. Soon the two families discovered that

Home and Family/81

their flocks were too large for the pasture fields around the mountain near Bethel. There was not enough grass for all the cattle.

Abram's shepherds wanted their flocks to have the best grass and plenty of water. Lot's shepherds wanted the same for their flocks.

Eventually Lot's herdsmen and Abram's herdsmen began to quarrel over the pastureland and water.

Abram was a peaceloving man. He did not like to hear the quarreling.

One day he called to his nephew. "Lot," said Uncle Abram. "I do not like the quarreling that is taking place between our herdsmen.

"Look at the land that is before you. Choose the section you want. Take your flocks and your herdsmen there. I will take whatever land is left. You make the first choice."

Lot looked around. He saw a beautiful green valley that was watered by the Jordan River. It had the appearance of a beautiful garden. The valley reminded Lot of the beauties of Egypt. My cattle would have plenty of grass in the valley, Lot must have thought.

"Uncle Abram," Lot said. "I will take the beautiful Jordan Valley that is covered with plenty of grass."

"It is yours," replied Uncle Abraham.

Soon Lot took his flocks and moved into the valley. The families were at peace with each other.

Response: Ask: "Which face would best describe the families when the story ended? Why were the families happy?

"Does this story give you an idea of something that you can do to help make your family happy? What can you do?

"Let's ask God to help us let others have first choice rather than our getting first choice all the time."

Prayer: Dear God. Help us be peacemakers with our family by not always wanting to get our way. Help us to let others have first choice. In Jesus' name, amen.

34
Being Obedient to My Parents

Preparation: Read Luke 2:41-52.

Sermon: Say, "I am thinking of a Bible verse that says, 'Children, obey your parents.' Say that verse with me.

"Listen to the story about Jesus and tell me whether or not Jesus was an obedient child."

Jesus was on his way to Jerusalem. Traveling to and from Jerusalem was fun as families and friends traveled together.

Jesus was very happy. Now that he was twelve, he was a "son of the law." That meant that he would get to go inside the Temple with the men and celebrate the Passover with them. The women—wives, mothers, sisters, and daughters—celebrated the Passover outside the Temple in a court.

The crowds gathered at Jerusalem. The festivities of the Passover began. Smoke rose from the burning sacrifices on the altars.

All too soon the celebration ended. Families and friends grouped together and started toward home.

All day they traveled. At sunset Mary and Joseph began making preparations to bed down for the night. They went looking for Jesus whom they thought was with friends and relatives. They looked and looked. "Have you seen Jesus?" they asked. They searched everywhere they knew to search, but could not find him.

Only one thing remained for them to do. They would return to Jerusalem and search for him there.

Back in Jerusalem, Mary and Joseph searched and looked. Where could Jesus be. For three days they hunted for him.

At last they found him. He was in the Temple. All that time Jesus had been in the Temple talking with the wisest men in the land who were students of the Scriptures. The teachers could hardly believe the deep understanding that Jesus had of the Scriptures. He could ask questions that even the wise teachers found difficult to answer.

When Mary and Joseph found him, they too were amazed.

"Son," his mother said, "why have you treated us this way? Your father and I have frantically searched everywhere for you."

"Why did you have to search for me? Did you not think that I would be here in the Temple?" Jesus replied.

Soon the three returned to Nazareth where Jesus obeyed them every day.

The obedient son grew tall and wise and was loved by God and by all who knew him.

Response: Ask: "Did Jesus obey his parents? Do you think that Jesus helped make his home happy by obeying his parents? Do you make your home a happy place when you obey?"

Prayer: Dear God. Help us be like Jesus by obeying our parents. In Jesus' name, amen.

35
Being Helpful to My Family

Preparation: Read Exodus 2:1-10.

Sermon: Ask: "How many of you have a job to do at home? What do you do? Do you find that things go better at your home when you do your chores?

"I will tell you a story about a child who helped at home. As I tell the story, I want you to think about what could have happened had the child not helped."

"What will we do with our beautiful new baby?" Amram and Jochebed must have asked each other. "He is too beautiful to throw in the Nile River."

You see, the Egyptian ruler Pharaoh had said that all Hebrew baby boys were to be thrown into the Nile River. The baby girls could live. Pharaoh was afraid that the Hebrews might someday become enemies of the Egyptians. Destroying all the baby boys would keep them from getting too strong, he thought.

"I know what I will do," Mother Jochebed decided. "I will hide my baby boy, and no one will know about him."

Jochebed, Amram, Aaron, and Miriam all kept the secret. No one must know about the new baby.

The baby grew and became larger and louder. Soon he was too big to hide.

Mother Jochebed thought of another plan. She gathered reeds that grew in the shallow water. Carefully she began to weave the reeds. Soon she had created a small, boat-like basket just large enough to hold her baby boy. Then she covered both the inside and outside of the basket with a tar-like substance.

"Come, Miriam," she probably said. "I have a job I want you to do."

Miriam obeyed. She followed her mother. Down the path that led to the river they went. Mother Jochebed carried her baby in the basket. Do you suppose Miriam wondered about what her mother planned to do?

When they reached the water's edge, Jochebed put the little boat basket in the water among the reeds and bullrushes that were growing there.

"Miriam," she said. "I want you to hide close by and watch your brother." Then she returned home.

Soon Miriam saw some people coming toward the water. It was the princess, the daughter of Pharaoh. She was coming with her servants to bathe in the river.

I wonder if Miriam's heart beat faster when she saw the approaching princess.

It was not long before the princess discovered the basket. "Go get the basket for me," she instructed a servant. When she opened the basket, the tiny baby began to cry. "This baby must belong to one of the Hebrews," she said.

Quickly Miriam ran to the princess. "Would you like for me to get someone to take care of the baby for you?" Miriam asked.

The princess consented. Quickly Miriam ran home and got her mother. The princess gave the baby to Jochebed and asked her to care for him.

Response: Ask: "What do you think would have happened had Miriam refused to help her mother?

"Boys and girls, what happens at your home when you do your chores, especially when you do them without fussing and grumbling? What happens when you refuse to do your chores?

"Someone suffers. Someone has to do their work plus yours. Do you think that is fair?

"Let's ask God to help us to make our home a happy place by doing our chores willingly and happily."

Prayer: Dear God. Thank you for homes. Thank you for helping us make our homes happy. Doing our chores is sometimes difficult—especially doing them willingly and cheerfully. Help us to be like Miriam and joyfully help at our home. In Jesus' name, amen.

Relationships

36
Learning About Sharing

Preparation: Read 2 Kings 5.
Get something to share with each child, such as pieces of candy, sticks of gum, or pennies.

Sermon: Give each child that which you brought to share. Ask, "Have I shared with you today? What did I share? How did I share?"

Say, "Today's story is about someone who shared. Find out who it was and what the person shared. Also listen to discover what happened as a result of the sharing."

Captain Naaman was sick. He had a terrible disease called leprosy. Leprosy was a disease of the skin that eventually brought death to the one who had it.

A little Jewish girl worked for Captain Naaman and his wife. When she discovered that Captain Naaman had leprosy, she thought about a man of God who lived near her back in Israel. I will share what I know, she must have thought.

The little girl talked with Captain Naaman's wife. She said: "I wish that my master would go see a prophet who lives in Samaria. The prophet could cure my master."

This news reached the king of Syria. "Captain Naaman," the

king said, "you go visit this prophet. I will write a letter that will introduce you to the king of Israel.

Soon Captain Naaman was on his way to see the prophet. He carried the letter and gifts of gold, silver, and fine robes.

When Naaman reached Israel, he presented his letter to the king. The king read these words: "The man who brought this letter to you is my servant Naaman. He has leprosy. I want you to heal him of this dreadful disease."

The king was furious. "Am I God? Can I kill and give life? This man sends me one sick of leprosy to heal! It is a trick. He is trying to get trouble started," the king said angrily.

Elisha, the prophet, learned about the angry king. "Send Naaman to me," Elisha requested. "I will teach him that there is a prophet of God in Israel."

Naaman left the king and drove to Elisha's house in a horse-drawn chariot.

Elisha sent his servant to tell Naaman to go wash seven times in the Jordan River.

How angry Naaman became. "Are not the rivers back in my home country just as good as the Jordan?" he asked.

Naaman's officers tried to reason with him. "Listen!" they said, "if the prophet had asked you to do something great, would you not have done it? This request is very simple—merely wash and be cured."

Captain Naaman thought about how childish he had acted. Then he started toward the dirty Jordan. He dipped himself seven times in the water. On the seventh emersion, a miracle happened. Captain Naaman's skin returned to its normal color. He was cured.

Happily Captain Naaman returned home. He was happy because he was cured.

Think about what happened, just because a little servant girl shared some good news.

Relationships/89

Response: Ask: "Who shared? What did she share? With whom did she share? What were the results of her sharing?

"Do you have something you can share with someone? Remember that it does not have to be something that you can hold in your hand or see. Let's name some things you can share." (Give time for responses.)

Prayer: Thank you, God, for sharing so many things with us. Help each of us to share something with someone else. That is a good way to be happy. In Jesus' name, amen.

37
Learning About Kindness

Preparation: Study Luke 10:29-37.

Find pictures of children doing unkind things. (Look through a teaching picture file in a children's Sunday School department.)

Sermon: Say: "I know a Bible verse that says, 'Be ye kind one to another.' Will you say the verse with me?

"Today, as I tell you a story, discover who showed kindness to another and what kindness he showed."

One day a man left the city of Jerusalem and started toward the city of Jericho. Before reaching his desired destination a terrible thing happened to him. Robbers attacked him. They took all of his clothes. They viciously beat him and then left him by the roadside almost dead.

The poor hurt man needed someone to help him. He needed someone to show him some kindness.

Before long, footsteps were heard. Would those sounds be coming from a person who would offer help and assistance to the injured man?

Surely he would receive help and attention because a priest was coming down the road. Surprisingly enough, the priest merely looked at the hurting man. He did not come close to him for he passed him by on the other side of the road. No assistance or help was offered.

By and by the sound of footsteps was heard again. Who would appear on the scene this time? Would this person bring help to the injured man?

A Levite followed the path of the priest. Now a Levite was a religious worker. A Levite was a servant of the priests. Sometimes they were in charge of music for worship.

Surely, this religious worker would show kindness to the hurt man. But oddly enough, he too did just as the priest had done. He showed no sympathy, no concern, no kindness. He merely looked at the hurting man and passed him by on the other side of the road.

Time passed. Sounds of footsteps were heard again. However, this time the sounds were different because they were the sounds of a walking animal.

Sure enough, an animal came down the road. Upon him rode a Samaritan. The Jews and the Samaritans were not friends. In fact, the Jews had no dealings with the Samaritans. Besides, the Samaritans were half-breeds.

Surely the hurt man will receive no compassion and help from the Samaritan.

Something very strange happened. The Samaritan stopped the animal. He got off the animal and knelt beside the hurting man. The Samaritan poured oil and wine into the open wounds and wrapped them in bandages. Carefully, he lifted the injured man onto the beast and walked along beside him.

Eventually they came to an inn. All that night the Samaritan cared for the sick one. The next morning, he paid the innkeeper and said: "Take care of him. If this is not enough money, I will pay you more the next time I am here."

Response: Ask, "Who was the kind man? How was he kind?" Show the pictures of children doing unkind things. Ask the group to study each picture and tell how the unkind child could show kindness. (Seek to show pictures that will speak to several areas of the children's lives.)

Prayer: Dear God. Many times it is hard to be kind. But help us all to show kindness to someone this next week. In Jesus' name, amen.

38
Learning About Honesty

Preparation: Read Joshua 7.

Sermon: Say, "I am thinking of one of the Ten Commandments that tells what one should not do with that which belongs to another. Can you say that Commandment for me? (*Thou shalt not steal.*)

"Listen to the story and discover the hurt that can take place whenever someone steals."

"When you fight the battle of Jericho, destroy everything. But all the silver and gold and vessels of brass and iron are consecrated unto the Lord. You must bring those items into his treasury," the Lord commanded.

Joshua's army marched around the city. The priests blew the trumpets and the army shouted. A loud crashing noise was heard. Rumblings of falling stone shook the earth. The walls of Jericho lay in ruins.

Joshua and his army won a victory.

Ai, a small city, had to be taken.

Joshua sent a group of men to spy on the city. They reported that the city was so small that only a part of the army would be needed to destroy it.

What a surprise Joshua had. The army of Ai swept down the hill and chased Joshua's soldiers far into the valley. Those who were not killed ran back to camp.

"Lord God, why have you let this happen to us?" Joshua questioned.

"The reason your army was defeated is because you have disobeyed me and have kept for yourselves treasure from Jericho. Someone has taken that which I said was not to be taken. You must find out who did it and punish him," God said.

The next morning all the tribes of Israel marched in front of Joshua. The Lord pointed out the tribe, the clan, and the family the guilty man belonged to.

Achan was guilty.

"Tell me what you have done," demanded Joshua.

Achan said: "I have sinned against the Lord God of Israel. I saw a beautiful robe that had come from Babylon. I saw some silver coins and a bar of gold. I so much wanted them. So I took them. I dug a hole in the earth under my tent and there hid the stolen treasure."

Joshua sent some men to search for the stolen items. Sure enough, they found everything to be just as Achan told.

But stealing and lying did not pay. Achan did not get to keep his treasure. Men died because of his disobedience. The army

Relationships/93

lost a battle. And Achan lost his life because his punishment was death.

Response: Ask: "Do you suppose that Achan thought that he could steal and not get caught? Do you suppose that boys and girls who steal think the same thing? Did you ever cheat in school and think that you would not get caught?

"Who knew all the time about Achan's dishonesty?

"Did Achan's stealing make good things happen?

"So it is with you. Nothing good will ever come from your stealing and dishonesty. However, dishonesty can cause lots of trouble and sadness."

Prayer: Dear God. Even though we may be tempted at times to take things that do not belong to us, help us to be honest and not steal. In Jesus' name, amen.

39
Learning About Caring for the Body

Preparation: Read Daniel 1.

Find pictures to represent ways to care for the body such as proper diet, exercise, and rest.

Sermon: Ask: "Has your mother ever said: 'Be sure to eat everything on your plate. The food is good for you. It will help make you grow.'

"Today our story is about a young man who was told to eat but who refused to do so. Listen to discover what happened to him."

The army of Babylon had captured Jerusalem. King Nebuchadnezzar took King Jehoiakim as prisoner. King Nebuchadnezzar also carried with him some golden vessels from the Temple in Jerusalem and put them before a heathen god in Babylon. Some of the finest youths of Jerusalem were also carried away as captives—youths who were handsome, intelligent, and energetic.

Daniel, Shadrach, Meshach, and Abednego were among the youths carried into captivity.

"Train these young men," said King Nebuchadnezzar to his steward. "Give them the best education possible. Teach them for three years and then bring them to me," he said.

The king wanted the young men to have the best. He instructed the steward to feed them rich food and good wine—the same that the king ate and drank.

When Daniel saw the food and drink that was set before him, he remembered what he had been taught about what to eat and what not to eat. I will have nothing to do with the king's food and drink, he thought.

Daniel talked with the steward. "Do not require us to eat the king's meat and drink the king's drink," he said.

The steward liked Daniel very much and wanted to honor Daniel's request. But the steward said, "I am afraid that you will not grow as you should. When you appear before the king who has commanded that you be fed this food and are weaker than the others, he will get rid of me."

"Experiment," said Daniel. "For ten days give us vegetables to eat and water to drink. Then compare us with the others who eat the king's rich food. Then decide which is best for us."

The steward agreed. For ten days Daniel and his friends ate vegetables and drank water.

When the ten days were up, Daniel and his friends appeared before the steward, along with the youths who had eaten the king's food. It so happened that Daniel, Shadrach, Meshach, and Abednego looked better and were fatter than those who had eaten the king's rich food.

Daniel had proven his point. The steward took away the rich food. He took away the wine they were to drink and gave them vegetables instead.

God helped the four young men grow strong in body and wise in their thinking.

The three years passed. The king commanded that the youths be brought before him. He found that Daniel and his friends were ten times wiser than all the wise men in the kingdom.

Response: Ask: "Were Daniel and his friends wise to eat good food? Why?"

Say: "God has given to each of you a body. He wants you to properly care for your body. Look at these pictures and tell me what they say to you about how you are to care for the body God has given you." (Show each picture and briefly discuss each one.)

Prayer: Dear God. In the Bible you have called our bodies a temple. Help each of us be wise like Daniel and his friends. Help us to take care of the body you have given to us. In Jesus' name, amen.

40
Learning to Accept Authority

Preparation: Read Philemon and Colossians 4:7-9.

Find pictures of a doctor, a schoolteacher, a policeman, parents, a Sunday School teacher and/or pastor.

96/A Year of Children's Sermons

Sermon: Say: "Boys and girls, I will show you some pictures of people that you often see. Tell me whether you should obey these people and why."

After the discussion say, "Listen to the story about a man who found obeying a very difficult thing to do."

For two years Paul had been a prisoner in Rome. He had been placed under house arrest when he first arrived in the city. Though he was free to have his friends visit with him, Paul was not free to leave the house. Roman soldiers probably guarded him at all times.

Among his many visitors was Onesimus, a runaway slave.

Onesimus had been the slave of Philemon from Colossae. One day while working for Philemon, Onesimus ran away. He might have stolen some money from Philemon to use after he escaped.

Onesimus traveled to many distant lands. Finally, he arrived in Rome. There he met Paul. They became good friends, and soon Onesimus became a Christian.

Paul liked Onesimus very much. "I would really like to keep you with me," Paul said, "but that would not be right." Paul knew that as a runaway slave Onesimus would have no future in the Roman world. He must encourage Onesimus to return to his master and to ask for forgiveness.

Paul knew that if Onesimus returned to Philemon, he would be taking a tremendous risk. Philemon could treat him with extreme cruelty. He could even have him killed.

Onesimus was afraid. But he knew that returning to his master was the right thing to do.

To protect the young man, Paul wrote a letter to Philemon. He asked Philemon to forgive the runaway slave and to receive him back into his household—not as a slave but as a Christian brother. Paul told Philemon how much he liked Onesimus. "I really wanted to keep him here with me while I am in prison," he wrote. "But I did not want to do it without your consent."

When Paul finished the letter, it was delivered to Philemon. Onesimus realized the danger involved. But he knew that he had done wrong, and he wanted to make that wrong right.

Although the Bible doesn't tell us what happened, many people believe that Philemon received Onesimus, forgave him, and set him free.

Response: Say, "I am thinking of a Bible verse that says, 'Obey your leaders' (Heb. 13:17, RSV). Will you say that verse with me?

"God wants you to listen to and obey the people that can help you do things that God wants you to do.

"Have you listened to and obeyed your Sunday School teachers? Your parents? Your pastor?"

Prayer: Dear God. Obeying our leaders is sometimes not easy to do. Help us to listen to them. Help us to obey them and do things that are right. In Jesus' name, amen.

41
Thou Shalt Not Covet

Preparation: Read 1 Kings 21.

Get a colorful catalog. Identify pages that picture items that are especially appealing to children.

Sermon: Show the catalog to the children.

Ask: "What do I have? What is a catalog? Do you enjoy looking at catalogs? Do you ever wish for things that you see pictured in a catalog?

"Today I will tell you a story about a man who wished for something that did not belong to him. Listen to find out what happened."

King Ahab looked at the field of grapes that grew near his house. I sure would like to have that land, he thought. I will go and talk with Naboth the Jezreelite. He owns the vineyard. Maybe I can trade him some land for that vineyard or even buy the land from him. I must have that land! I must! reasoned Ahab.

So Ahab spoke to Naboth. "Give me your vineyard," Ahab said. "It is near my house and I want to plant a garden of herbs on it. I will trade you a better vineyard for it. Or, if you wish, I will pay you for the land. Which offer will you accept?"

"Neither," replied Naboth. "This land belonged to my father, my grandfather, and to his father before him. It now belongs to me. I do not want to sell it."

Ahab was very disappointed. He did not like what he had heard. Naboth's refusal to sell or trade made Ahab angry.

Ahab returned to his house. He was so displeased that he went to bed. He would not talk with anyone and he refused to eat.

"Ahab, what is wrong with you?" questioned Queen Jezebel. "Why have you gone to bed? Why are you pouting? Why do you refuse to eat? What is wrong?"

"Naboth refused to sell or trade the land that I want. He told me that he would not give me his vineyard," Ahab complained.

"Who is the King of Israel?" Queen Jezebel asked. "Get out of the bed. Eat your meals and be happy because I will get the vineyard for you."

Jezebel immediately began to put her evil plan into action. She wrote letters and sent them to the important men who lived in Naboth's town.

"Have a celebration. Make sure that Naboth is one of the leaders of the celebration. Ask two men to tell lies on him by saying that Naboth cursed God and the king. Then drag him outside the city and stone him to death," she wrote.

Jezebel signed the letters. Rather than signing her name, she signed the king's name and sealed the letters with the king's seal.

The men received the letters and obeyed the evil instructions. Naboth was killed.

When Jezebel learned that Naboth was dead, she went to the king and said: "Arise, take possession of the vineyard of Naboth, which he refused to give you for money: for Naboth is not alive. He is dead."

Response: Say, "Ahab and Jezebel wanted so badly something that belonged to someone else that they were willing to do anything to get it. The Bible calls that coveting.

"God said: 'Thou shalt not covet—wish so much for something that belongs to another that you will do wrong to get it.'

"Wishing is not bad. But when you are willing to do wrong to get the things for which you wish, then wishing becomes bad.

"Say God's law with me."

Prayer: Dear God, help us to wish for things but help us to always want to do right. Help us to never be willing to do wrong in order to get that for which we wish. In Jesus' name, amen.

42
Learning About Doing One's Best

Preparation: Study Genesis 37—41.

On a piece of poster board print, "God wants me to always do my best." First, print the sentence the best you can. Carelessly print the sentence the second time beneath the carefully printed sentence.

Sermon: Show the poster. Ask the children to read the sentence. Tell them that you printed both sentences. Ask them to identify the one you printed as best you could and the one that you printed carelessly.

Ask, "Have your teachers, parents, or friends ever said to you, 'Do your best'?"

"Today, I will tell you a story about a boy who was not told to do his best. Listen and discover what happened to him."

Joseph was far from home. He was probably lonely. He might have been sad because his brothers were the cause of his being in Egypt. They sold him to a caravan of traders who sold him to Captain Potiphar, head of the palace guard.

"I do not want to work! I do not like being a slave! I'll just do what I have to do and no more," Joseph could have thought.

But that was not the case. Joseph did his very best in every chore he was assigned. He worked carefully, faithfully, and thoroughly. His work was so good that Captain Potiphar made Joseph head of all the house servants.

Joseph continued to work well. Soon Captain Potiphar put Joseph in charge of the work that was done outside the house in the fields.

Because Joseph continued to do his best and to work so well, Captain Potiphar promoted Joseph to be responsible for all the captain's business.

Things went well until Captain Potiphar believed a lie that his wife told about Joseph. Captain Potiphar became so angry with Joseph that he put Joseph in jail.

"Look at what doing my best has brought to me! A home, yes! But who wants to live in a jail?" Joseph could have said.

That must not have happened. He worked in jail just as faithfully and just as well as he had worked in Potiphar's house. Soon the jailer learned that he could depend on Joseph. The jailer gave Joseph so many important things to do that soon he was in charge of all the prisoners.

One day Joseph was taken from jail to Pharaoh's palace. Pharaoh was the ruler over Egypt. "I have dreamed and no one can tell me what my dreams mean. I hear that you can interpret dreams," said Pharaoh.

"God gives me understanding. I only tell what God tells me," responded Joseph.

Joseph listened to Pharaoh tell his dreams about corn and cattle. Then Joseph said: "For seven years crops will grow well and produce much. The next seven years very little will grow.

"Put someone in charge of storing grain during the seven years of plenty," Joseph advised.

Suddenly many new things happened to Joseph. Pharaoh made Joseph the governor of Egypt.

Response: Discuss what might have happened had Joseph not done his best.

Lead the group to say, "Whatever you do, do well" (Eccl. 9:10, TLB).

Prayer: Dear God, even though many times we do not want to, help us to always do well that which we do. In Jesus' name, amen.

43
Learning About Heroes

Preparation: Read Daniel 3.

Sermon: Ask: "What person do you know whom you think is a hero? What makes that person a hero?

"I will tell you a story about three men. Listen and decide whether or not these men were heroes."

King Nebuchadnezzar made a huge golden statue. It was ninety feet tall and nine feet wide. He placed the statue on the flat lands in Babylon so that the people could easily see it.

King Nebuchadnezzar sent letters to all the important people in his kingdom. "Come to the Plain of Dura. We will worship the golden statue."

Great crowds of people gathered. The king's herald shouted, "O people of all nations and languages, this is the king's command:

"When the band strikes up, you are to fall flat on the ground to worship King Nebuchadnezzar's golden statue; anyone who refuses to obey will immediately be thrown into a flaming furnace" (Dan. 3:5-6, TLB).

The band began to play. Everyone—well, almost everyone—fell to the ground and worshiped the big, golden statue. Shadrach, Meshach, and Abednego refused to obey the king's command. They were Jews. They had been taught to neither make, bow down before, or serve graven images.

Someone ran to tell the king. "Shadrach, Meshach, and Abednego have refused to obey your law," they said.

King Nebuchadnezzar became very angry. "Bring them to me," he commanded.

"Is it true," the king asked the three men, "that you have disobeyed my command and have refused to serve my gods and worship the golden statue? I will give you one more chance. When you hear the music, fall to the ground and worship the statue or you will be thrown into the flaming furnace."

"O Nebuchadnezzar," said Shadrach, Meshach, and Abednego, "we are not worried. Our God is able to deliver us. And even though he doesn't, we will not serve your gods nor bow to your golden statue."

King Nebuchadnezzar's face expressed fierce anger. He commanded that the furnace be made seven times hotter than usual. He had Shadrach, Meshach, and Abednego bound and thrown into the furnace.

The king watched. "Did we not throw three men in the furnace?" he asked. "I see four men walking in the fire. The fourth man looks like the Son of God."

Nebuchadnezzar walked to the furnace. He called for the three Hebrews to come out.

The three walked from the furnace. Their clothes were not burned neither did they have the smell of smoke.

The king rejoiced! He made another decree that said: "Anyone who speaks against the God of Shadrach, Meshach, and Abednego will be punished."

Response: Ask: "Were Shadrach, Meshach and Abednego heroes? Why?"

"Do you know that you can be a hero? In fact, most of you, if not all of you, are heroes.

"When you are tempted to disobey God but do not disobey him, you become a hero."

Prayer: Thank you, God, for heroes. Help each of us to do what you want us to do. Help us to be heroes. In Jesus' name, amen.

44
Learning About Fears

Preparation: Read Matthew 8:18-27; Luke 24:36-43.
Recall a frightening experience that you had as a child. Prepare to tell the experience to the children.

Sermon: Ask, "How many of you have ever been afraid?

"I remember one time, when as a child, I became afraid. (Relate the experience.)

"I will tell you two short stories. In each story a group of men became afraid. Each time, however, something happened that helped them. Listen to discover what happened."

"Get ready to cross over to the other side of the lake," Jesus instructed his disciples. Preparations were made.

Jesus got into the boat with his disciples, and they started across the lake.

He had had a very busy day. He must have been tired and weary for soon he was asleep.

Suddenly the wind began to blow. Hard and strong it blew. The waves began to beat upon the boat. The waves got higher and higher. Water began to fill the boat. The storm grew so bad that the disciples became scared. They were afraid the boat might sink and they would all drown in the lake.

They made their way to Jesus. "Lord, save us! Wake up! Teacher, do you not care that we perish? Wake up! We are going to drown!" they shouted frantically.

Jesus awoke. He looked at the frightened men. Then he said: "Why are you so frightened? Oh! you have so little faith."

Then amid all the strong wind and beating waves, Jesus stood. He looked out into the storm. With the ring of authority in his voice, he said: "Peace! Be still!"

Immediately the winds obeyed his command. So did the waves. A calm peace hovered over the lake.

The disciples were very much surprised. They could hardly believe what had happened.

"Who is this person?" they asked. "Even the winds and the waves obey him."

Another time the disciples were together. Jesus was not with them. He had been crucified. However, some men from Emmaus were telling about having seen the resurrected Lord. Just as they told their story, Jesus himself suddenly appeared and stood among them. He spoke to them but fear came upon the entire group. They all thought they were seeing a ghost.

"Why are you afraid? Why do you doubt that I am real? Look at my hands and my feet. Handle me and know that I am not a ghost. Ghosts do not have flesh and bones," he said.

Although joyful, the disciples still doubted. "Have you anything to eat?" Jesus asked.

The disciples gave him a piece of fish and some honey. They watched him as he ate.

Then Jesus had a good time visiting with his friends. He explained many Scripture verses to them. Their fear disappeared.

Response: Ask, "Who helped the disciples in their times of fright? *(Jesus.)*

"The shepherd David must have sometimes been afraid. He wrote, 'What time I am afraid, I will trust in thee' (Ps. 56:3). Say that verse with me.

"The next time something happens that frightens you, think about God. The Bible does not say that you will no longer be afraid, but thinking about God will somehow help you better face your fears."

Prayer: Thank you, God, for telling us to trust you when we are afraid. Help us to know how to do that. In Jesus' name, amen.

45
Learning About Jealousy

Preparation: Study Daniel 6.

Sermon: Ask, "Can you think of anyone who can do something better than you?

"Today, I will tell you about a man who did things better than the people with whom he worked. Listen to discover what happened."

King Darius chose 120 princes to be in charge of the entire kingdom. He appointed three presidents to be in charge of the princes.

Daniel was one of the presidents. He had greater ability and was more capable than the other presidents. In fact, he did his work so well that the king thought about putting him in charge of everyone.

The other two presidents became jealous of Daniel.

"Let's watch him very carefully and find fault in something he does," they said. Even though they carefully watched him, they could find nothing to criticize. He was faithful to the king. He was honest, and he did nothing that was wrong.

Then the two presidents thought of a mean and cruel plan. Hurriedly they went to the king. "King Darius, may you live forever," they said. "All the presidents, princes, counselors, and captains of the kingdom have agreed that you should make a law that cannot be broken under any circumstance. The law should say that for the next thirty days no one shall ask a favor of God or man except from you. He who does shall be thrown into the den of lions."

Not knowing what the presidents were trying to do, King Darius made the law. He signed it which made it unchangeable.

When Daniel learned of the law, he went home and prayed to his God, just as he did three times each day.

The presidents and princes caught Daniel praying and reported Daniel's action to the king.

King Darius became very upset with himself for having signed such a law when he learned that Daniel had disobeyed. The rest of that day he tried to think of some way to save Daniel from the lions. He was unsuccessful.

That night the king could not sleep. All night he worried about Daniel. Early the next morning, he hurried to the lions' den.

"Daniel! Daniel!" he called. "Is your God able to save you?"

"May you live forever, King Darius," Daniel replied. "My God sent an angel and shut the lions' mouths."

King Darius was overjoyed. He released Daniel from the lions' den. He examined him to see if he had been hurt in any way. He could not find even as much as a scratch.

Then the king gave an order for all the men who accused Daniel to be punished. Afterwards he made another decree which read, "Daniel's God is to be worshiped everywhere in all the kingdom!"

Response: Ask: "How did the men who worked with Daniel feel about him? What caused them to have bad feelings toward Daniel? (*They were jealous.*)

"Do you remember some of the bad things that jealousy caused? (*Plotting, tattling, lying, killing, destroying a person.*)

"Boys and girls, remember that jealousy can make you do bad and mean things. So be very careful about your feelings toward others."

Prayer: Dear God. Jealousy can make us do things that are mean and wrong. Help each of us to have loving attitudes toward others. In Jesus' name, amen.

46
Learning About Mercy

Preparation: Read Joshua 2; 6.

Sermon: Say: "One day Jesus said, 'Blessed are the merciful: for they shall obtain mercy'" (Matt. 5:7).

"Say that verse with me.

"Now let's talk about what the verse means. The word *mercy* means kindness. The word *obtain* means to get. Therefore, Jesus was saying that if you are kind to others, others will in return be kind to you.

"Listen to the story and discover who it was that showed mercy."

The children of Israel were getting ready to cross over the Jordan River into the land that God had promised them.

Just across the river was the city of Jericho. Having a king, an army, and strong high walls, its people felt secure and protected.

"In order to possess the land, we must conquer that city," thought Joshua. "I must know how strong Jericho really is."

Joshua chose two men to go as spies. Their orders were to slip into Jericho and discover how strong the city really was.

Across the river they went. Straight to the city of Jericho they walked. Because the city gates were open during the day, they encountered no difficulty in getting inside.

Within the city, they found a house built on the city wall. A friendly woman named Rahab lived there.

Thinking they would need a place to stay at night, the spies asked her to let them stay in her house. She agreed.

The king learned that two strange men were in the city. Immediately the king's soldiers began to hunt for the men.

On the roof, Rahab was drying stacks of flax to use in making cloth.

"Hide under the flax," Rahab urged the spies.

The king's soldiers searched Rahab's house. They also searched across the fields, but they did not find the strangers.

That night, Rahab went up on the roof. She said to the spies: "I know about you and your God. I know what your God has done for your people. He is the true God of heaven and earth. Our entire city is scared of you.

"Promise to show me kindness as I have shown you kindness. When you come back to capture the city, please do not harm me nor my family.

The spies promised safety for Rahab and her family.

In the darkness of the night, Rahab helped the spies escape. She put a rope out of one of her windows. The spies slid down the rope on the outside of the wall.

"Keep this red rope hanging from your window," whispered the spies. "That will be the sign for our army to protect you."

Sure enough, a few days later the Israelite army surrounded the city.

Once every day, for five days, the army marched around the city. On the sixth day, they marched around the city six times. Upon command, the soldiers shouted and the priests blew their trumpets.

Suddenly the high, strong walls of Jericho crumbled and fell. However, not all of the wall fell. From a window in the section of the wall that still remained, hung a red rope.

Rahab and her family were protected and saved from death.

Response: Ask: "Who showed mercy? Was mercy shown to them? How? How can you show mercy to your school friends this week?"

Prayer: Dear God. Help each of us to be quick to show mercy toward others. Help us to learn each day how to be kind. In Jesus' name, amen.

Special Days

47
Thanking God for Mothers

Preparation: Read through the Gospels accounts and refresh your memory about qualities that Mary, the mother of Jesus, possessed.

Sermon: Say, "One day a little boy in kindergarten said, 'My mommy is the best mommy in the whole world.' I am sure that many of you feel much the same way about your mothers. What about your mothers do you like best? (Give adequate time for responses.)

"Today I want us to think about one of the mothers in the Bible—Mary, the mother of Jesus.

"Listen to the story. Be able to tell me some things about the mother of Jesus that you like."

Mary lived in the little town of Nazareth. She and Joseph, the carpenter, were engaged to be married.

One day an unusual visitor came to see her. His presence made her afraid. For you see, he was Gabriel, one of God's messengers.

"Do not be afraid, Mary," Gabriel said. "You have found favor with God. He has chosen you to be a very special mother. Very soon you will have a baby boy. You will name him Jesus. He will be very great. He will be called the Son of God."

Mary was very confused. "How can I have a baby?" she ques-

Special Days/111

tioned. "I am not married."

"God will make all of this happen. Your baby boy will be God's Son," Gabriel answered.

"I am willing to do whatever God wants me to do," Mary said.

Mary needed to share the exciting news with someone. A few days later she left Nazareth to visit with her cousin Elizabeth. Elizabeth, too, was expecting a baby boy.

The two ladies visited and thanked God for being so good.

Mary must have known the Scriptures because she said to Elizabeth: "I will have the baby boy that God promised to our ancestors—Abraham and his family."

Time past. Mary and Joseph married. They went to Bethlehem on a business trip. While there, Mary's baby was born.

Shepherds came and worshiped the baby. "Angels told us about him," they reported. Mary quietly thought about all the things that were happening.

Mary was a religious woman. Each year she traveled with her family to Jerusalem to observe the religious feasts and celebrations.

Mary was a concerned mother. One day she and Joseph could not find Jesus. They worried about him and searched three days before finding him.

Mary believed in her family. She attended a wedding in Cana. Jesus and his disciples were there too. When the wedding party ran out of wine, she told the servants that Jesus could take care of the embarrassing situation. "Whatever he tells you to do, do it," she instructed.

Mary became a follower of her son, Jesus. She was at the foot of his cross the day he was crucified. And she was one of the believers who told others of Jesus after Jesus went back to heaven.

Mary was a wonderful mother.

Response: Ask, "What things about Mary, the mother of Jesus, do you like?"

Prayer: Dear God. Thank you for giving us mothers. Help us today to say to them, "I love you." In Jesus' name, amen.

48
O Give Thanks

Preparation: Read Exodus 14—15.
Print, in large letters, the word *T H A N K S*.

Sermon: Say: "This week we will celebrate a special day. What day is it? Why do we celebrate Thanksgiving?"

Show the word *thanks*. Say: "Think of things for which you are thankful that begin with the letters of this word. Let's name some of them. (Give adequate time for response. Start with the letter *T* and move quickly through the entire word.)

"I will tell you a story about a thanksgiving service that took place long before America was ever thought about. Listen to discover who had the service and why they were thankful."

Pharaoh only a few days before had told Moses to take the Hebrew slaves and leave Egypt.

The Hebrews had traveled as far as the Red Sea.

They were not aware that Pharaoh had changed his mind. He wanted the Hebrews back in Egypt to serve as slaves to the Egyptians. He followed them with an army and six hundred chariots of war.

When the Hebrews discovered that the Red Sea was in front of them and Pharaoh's army behind them, they began to complain to Moses.

"What have you done to us?" they cried. "Why have you brought us out here into the wilderness to die? It would have been better for us to have stayed in Egypt and served the Egyptians," they said.

"Do not be afraid," said Moses, their leader. "God will fight for you today. All you have to do is to be still."

"Tell the people to go forward," God said to Moses. "Lift your shepherd's rod and stretch it out over the sea."

Moses did as God had told him. He ordered the Hebrews to start moving forward. He stretched his shepherd's rod as far as he could stretch out over the sea.

Suddenly, God made a strong wind blow. The wind blew across the sea so forcefully that it made the waters separate. A dry path appeared in the middle of the sea.

Sure enough, God had provided a way for the Hebrews to escape slaughter from Pharaoh's army. Joyfully, the Hebrews marched through the sea.

The Egyptians saw the dry path. They thought that they too could do as the Hebrews. The chariots began to thunder across the path through the sea.

Something happened. The path was no longer dry. It became muddy and wet. Chariot wheels began to spin in the mud. Soon the mud got so deep that the chariot wheels could no longer roll.

By this time, all the Hebrews were safely across the sea.

"Stretch your hand across the sea, Moses," God said.

When Moses obeyed, the walls of water that stood on either side of the path immediately collapsed. The waters gushed together. Pharaoh's army was trapped. They drowned in the sea.

Moses was happy. His sister Miriam was happy. In fact, everyone was happy. They were so happy that they had a thanksgiving service on the banks of the Red Sea. Miriam led the women in playing their tambourines while the Hebrews sang a song of praise.

Response: Ask: "Who had a thanksgiving service on the banks of the Red Sea? Why?"

Prayer: God. We, too, are thankful. Accept our thanks we pray. In Jesus' name, amen.

49
He Is Alive

Preparation: Read Mark 16.

Sermon: Ask: "How many of you ever had a surprise? How did you feel? Have any of you ever had a surprise that frightened you?

"Today our story is about a series of surprises that a group of ladies had on the very first Lord's Day."

It was early Sunday morning. The sun had not come up. Three women were already up, dressed, and on their way to the tomb in the garden. They carried some very special spices they had bought. Soon they would pour those spices over Jesus' body. That was a burial custom in those days.

As they hurried along the path that lead to the tomb, they talked. Their conversation revealed the fact that they were worried. "Who will roll the large stone away from the tomb for us?" they questioned.

On the preceding Friday, Jesus had been crucified. Joseph from Arimathea and Nicodemus had buried Jesus in a rock tomb that belonged to Joseph. They rolled a large, heavy stone in front of the door of the tomb.

Just about sunrise, the ladies reached the garden. The soft

sunlight drove away all darkness.

When they looked, they were surprised! Someone had arrived before them and had already rolled the heavy stone away from the door of the tomb.

The ladies entered the tomb, thinking that they would find the body of Jesus. Rather, they received the greatest surprise of the morning. They looked for Jesus' body but could not find it. Instead, they found a strange visitor, sitting on the right side of the tomb. He was dressed in a robe of white—so white that it shone.

Fear came upon the women. They were scared. "Do not be afraid," said the white-robed visitor. "Are you looking for Jesus of Nazareth who was crucified? He is not here. He is no longer dead. He is alive! Come, look at the place where he was laid."

The angel continued. "Do not stay here. Go on your way. Give this message to the disciples and Peter: 'Jesus is going before you to Galilee. You will find him there, just as he told you before he was crucified.'"

Immediately the ladies ran from the tomb. They were so frightened that they trembled, but they were also filled with great joy.

Mary Magdalene shared the good news with the disciples who were sad and crying from grief. "He is alive!" she shouted joyfully. "He is alive!"

Response: Immediately after the second "He is alive!" have a choir (children's choir or adult choir) or a soloist to sing stanza one, "The First Lord's Day," *Baptist Hymnal*, 1975 edition, Number 119.

Prayer: Thank you, God, for Jesus who is still alive. Thank you for the first Lord's Day. Help us to remember that every Sunday as we celebrate the resurrection of Jesus our Savior and Lord. In whose name we pray, amen.

50
Learning the Meaning of Christmas

Preparation: Study the Christmas story as recorded in Matthew and Luke.

Print the word *C H R I S T M A S*. Print each letter on a separate piece of poster board or paper. Make them as attractive as possible

Sermon: Say: "This week we celebrate the birthday of Jesus. I like the time of the year. Do you? What about Christmas do you like? (Give adequate time for responses.)

"Now let me share some of the things about Christmas that I like. I will use the letters that spell Christmas and tell you what Christmas means to me."

Call for nine children to help you. After you use each letter, give the letter poster to a child to hold. Assist them in arranging the letters so that Christmas is spelled correctly.

C—C reminds me of Christ and child. Put the two words together and you have Christ child. The Christ child was born on Christmas day.

H—H makes me think about a herald. A herald is a person who carries messages and makes announcements. Remember the angel who visited the shepherds made an announcement. "Unto you is born this day in the city of David a Saviour which is Christ the Lord," announced the angel.

R—The letter R makes me think of the word *real.* Jesus was real. He really was a baby. He really did grow as a boy. He really did grow to be a man. He really was God's Son.

I—I helps me recall another name that was given to Jesus. He was known as Immanuel. The word Immanuel means, "God with us." Jesus was truly God. God, through Jesus, came to live with man.

S—S stands for shepherds. "And there were in the same country shepherds abiding in the field, keeping watch over their flock by night" (Luke 2:8). The angel told them about Jesus having been born. The shepherds went immediately and found the newborn baby.

T—T means tidings. Tidings means news or a message. To the shepherds the angel said: "Behold, I bring you good tidings of great joy. . . . For unto you is born this day in the city of David a Saviour which is Christ the Lord" (Luke 2:10-11).

M—M makes me think of manger. A manger is a box in which food for animals is placed. Jesus was born in a stable, a place where animals were kept. The Bible says that Mary wrapped Jesus in swaddling clothes and laid him in a manger.

A—A helps me think of angels. One angel visited the shepherds and told them about the birth of Jesus. After the angel finished telling the good news, a great army—a huge chorus—of angels filled the skies. Together they sang: "Glory to God in the highest, and on earth peace, good will toward men" (Luke 2:14).

S—The last letter of Christmas makes me think about another one of the great names given to Jesus. The name is Savior. The angel said of Jesus to Joseph, "He shall save his people from their sins" (Matt. 1:21).

Boys and girls, that is what Christmas means to me.

Response: Ask the congregation to stand and join the children in singing "Joy to the World! The Lord Is Come."

Prayer: Thank you, God, for sending Jesus. Thank you for Christmas, the time of the year when we celebrate Jesus' birthday. In whose name we pray, amen.

51
The Beginning of a Nation

Preparation: Study Genesis 12.

Get a birthday cake. If possible have red, white, and blue icing on it.

Sermon: Display the birthday cake. Mention the fact that this week our nation's birthday will be celebrated. Give a brief historical account of our nation's birth.

Say: "A story in the Bible tells about the birth of a special nation. Listen as I tell you about it. Find out the name of the man God used to start that nation and why God started the nation."

God had a plan. He had promised Adam and Eve that he would someday send a Savior to the world. The Savior would need a family. The family would need to be very special. They would need to trust and love God.

Far away in the city of Ur, God found a man whom he chose to start that special family. The man's name was Abram. It was later changed to Abraham.

God spoke to Abram. He said: "Abram, prepare to leave the country where you now live. Leave your relatives and your friends. Move to a land that I will show you.

"If you obey me, I will bless you. You will be the father of a great nation. Your name will become great. I will bless those who bless you and will curse those that curse you. If you obey me, all the nations of the earth will be blessed."

Although Abram did not know where God would lead him, he decided to obey.

Abram, his wife Sarai, Terah, his father, and Lot, Abram's nephew, packed their belongings and made ready for a long trip. Their destination they did not know.

Special Days/119

The family traveled north. They came to a place called Haran. They put up their tents and stayed there for awhile. While in Haran, Terah died.

"You have not yet reached the land I will give you," said God. "It is time to travel again."

This time Abram, Sarai, Lot and their servants and animals and flocks traveled south. At last they came to the land of Canaan.

God appeared to Abram and said, "This is the land that I will give you. It belongs to you and your family."

Although Abram at that time had no children, he believed what God told him. He built an altar and worshiped the God who had led him to this new land.

Time passed. Abram and Sarai grew old. They still had no children. They may have wondered if God would be true to his promise concerning a family. Sure enough, when Abram was one hundred years old and Sarai ninety, they had a baby boy. They named him Isaac.

That was the beginning of the special family that God needed in which his Son, the Savior, would be born.

Many, many years later Mary visited Elizabeth. Not long before, an angel had visited Mary and told her that she would have a baby boy. She was to name him Jesus for he would save his people from their sins. As Mary told Elizabeth the good news, she said: "God has not forgotten his promise that he made to our ancestor—Abraham and his children."

Mary was a part of Abraham's family. She was the mother of Jesus, the Savior.

Remember God's promise to Abraham—"You will become a great nation and all the nations of the world will be blessed."

Response: Call for brief answers to the two questions you posed before telling the story.

Prayer: Thank you, God, for Abraham and the special nation he started through which God sent Jesus. Thank you for our great nation that allows us this privilege of worshiping you. In Jesus' name, amen.

52
Thanking God for Fathers

Preparation: Read through the story of Abraham found in Genesis.

Prepare a poster board with the letters *F A T H E R* written as an acrostic starting at the top and progressing to the bottom of the left side.

Sermon: Say: "Today is a special day. We honor our fathers today. I suppose that most of you think that your father is a great guy! What about your fathers do you like best? (Give adequate time for responses.)

"I want us to think about one of the famous fathers in the Bible. His name is Abraham.

"To help you remember, I will use the word *father* as I tell you the story." (Display the poster and fill it in as appropriate while you tell the story.)

F—The letter *F* makes me think about the word faith. Abraham was a man of great faith and belief in God. Abraham grew up in the city of Ur. The people of that city worshiped the sun. God spoke to Abraham one day. "Abram, I want you to leave Ur and go to a land that I will show you." Even though Abraham had no idea where God might lead him, he willingly left Ur and eventually traveled to Canaan.

Special Days/121

A—A helps me think of altar. When one studies the life of Abraham, he discovers that Abraham built many altars and used them in his worship of God. Every time something special happened in the life of Abraham, he built an altar and worshiped.

T—T stands for Terah, the name of Abraham's father. It also stands for traveler, for that is what Abraham was. He traveled from Ur of the Chaldees to the faraway place of Haran to the south country of Canaan. From Canaan he traveled to Egypt and back.

H—H is for herds. Abraham was rich. He had treasures of silver and gold and many, many cattle, sheep, oxen, and camels. His nephew Lot also owned very large herds. In fact, Abraham divided the land that God gave to him between himself and his nephew. That way both of their herds had plenty to eat.

E—E stands for Eliezer. Eliezer was one of Abraham's servants. He went on a special errand for his master. After Sarah, Abraham's wife died, Abraham said to Eliezer, "Go back to Haran where we lived for awhile—back where my brother lives. There among my own people search out a wife for my son Isaac."

R—R is for Rebekah, the name of the beautiful girl who gave Eliezer and his camels a drink of water. She became Isaac's bride and Abraham's daughter-in-law.

Put the letters together and they spell *father*. Abraham was a father and is the father of the great nation—Israel. And just as God promised, through Abraham, all the nations of the world have been blessed.

Although Abraham was a great father and although your fathers are wonderful, the greatest father is God, our heavenly Father. Because we are his children, he cares for us and takes care of all of our needs.

Prayer: Thank you, God, for fathers. Thank you for being our heavenly Father. Thank you for letting us be your children. Thank you for all you do for us. In Jesus' name, amen.